Love In
The Belly of The Beast
an anthology

La Bruja

ISBN 9782957498437

©2021
Published by La Bruja

Cover Art By Eddie Jelinet

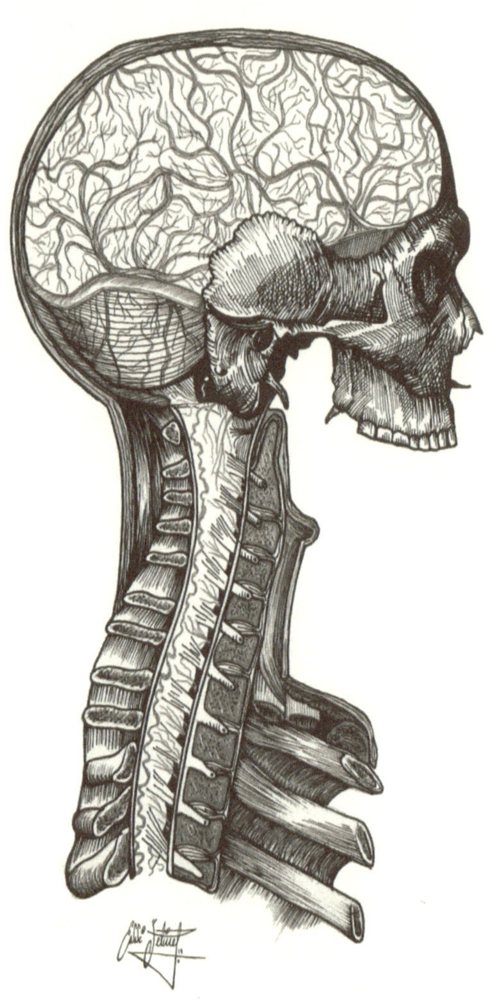

Rebellious Thoughts

I

A Moment of Silence

Let us take a moment of silence. Let us take a moment of silence for Syria, and for Iraq, for Palestine, for Algeria, for Rwanda, for Cameroon, for China, for Russia, for North America, for South America, for New York, for Hong Kong, for Mexico. Let us take a moment of silence for all the nations and for all the lands because word is we are all doomed. We are pressing the red button that will explode us into our great karmic paths and we will all be reborn the burnt particles of a lost world, a lost race, and a lost form.

All nature's cruelties seem to be the inevitable struggles, complexities, and sufferings of maintaining life. Yet, man races towards death. Man has no reverence, no desire for true life. Man is a coward bombing his way to extinction and denying it as he burns.

Let us take a moment of silence for all that is dying.

II

Do Not Be Fooled or Real Talk

Violence never equals peace. War is never a means to peace. War is an interruption of peace. War is war. Those who partake in any "justification" rhetoric are part of the problem. Those who send you off to kill the other in order to free the other, they are the problem.

The soldiers of Hollywood go out to conquer the world and to spin the deadly American dream into unsuspecting minds. Then the army, with their gas masks and bombs and tanks and their bogus banners of freedom will shortly follow. They will "liberate" your community from the mundaneness of simple life and they will swallow you into the agony of "the grind," "the rat race," "progress," and "freedom."

The American Dream, Hollywood, the smiles, the endless sunshine, the ease and comfort and acquisition... Do not buy into the propaganda. Those of us sunbathing in the belly of the beast are the first ones to burn in the hell of patriarchy. We are the first severed and dismembered, de-souled, and de-naturalized: colonized and now trying to maintain the great burden of being civilized.

Do not buy into the bleached smiles and bleached skins, and bleached, now spiritless brains. We are the first betrayed and now complicit in the infernal race to distinguish all life: anything that is not automated. We've been swallowed by the jaws of psychopaths and we are in a stupor: interior decorating our prisons, febreezing over the stench, and instant-gratificationizing the rotting soul.

Do not emulate the skeletons parading their vapid cruelty before your eyes, selling you romance and cigarettes and a good fuck. These people are dead. They've been digested by the rancid, intestinal highway of progress and false-superiority. Almost all instinct discarded, these people wallow in despair.

III

We Live

We are alive and multiplying. We: the artists, the livers, the lovers, the mothers, the fathers, the fighters, the huggers, the gardeners, the teachers, the dreamers, the listeners, the poets, the writers, the storytellers, the painters, the dancers. We who do not digest well, we live on. We. Our organic souls alight, our instinct rousing, we live on.

-A. Gallagher

Love in
The Belly of The Beast
Vol. II 2021

El Elixir

Tengo algo que decirte.
No sé a quién le servirá
pero necesito decir algo
a todos ustedes que se encuentran entre
la influencia de estas redes sociales.

Últimamente he sentido mucho a mirar
como las cosas están en estos tiempos. `
Anoche me enteré de quiénes son algunos de los
"aquellos,"
los "ellos" que hacen esto y el otro.
Ellos (they) – el 1% ...

Me da mucha rabia que la gente siga soportando
tantas cosas.
Pero la verdad es que algunos somos ciegos.
Así que deseo correr el velo de vuestros ojos
por si acaso sois uno de los ciegos.
Así deseo aclarar la vibración.
Me da mucha lastima saber de tantas mentiras,
de falsas apariencias,
de una sociedad enferma y ciega.
Pero no somos víctimas.
Ya no pretendo no saber.

Ahora veo.
Ahora oigo.
Por favor
dejen de pelear!
Dejen de tener miedo.

La sabiduría no miente.
Mírate en el espejo.
pregúntate ¿Por qué me perturba?
¿Por qué me frustra?
¿Por qué resisto?
¿Por qué permito que invadan mi paz interior?
¿Tenéis conciencia?
¿Tenemos conciencia?

Pregúntate a qué precio seguirás alimentando lo injusto,
alimentando miedos y trastornos.
¿A qué precio guardas esta oscuridad?

Oye, si alguna vez te acuerdas de mi
quiero decirte que te amo,
que nunca jamás tenéis que alimentar mentiras,
juicios, ni prejuicios.
Te lo digo de todo corazón.

No toméis el veneno.
No lo tomes.
No tomes odio, amargura,
culpa, pena, soledad, tristeza.

El odio es el veneno.
Procura mejor tomar
el elixir del Amor.

Cuando sientas aquella ira,
la que te urge la programación.
Cuando sientas aquello y sabes
que no es mentira lo que sientes.
Sabéis lo que sientes.
No creas que no.
No creas que estás loca.
No creas que no vale la pena.
Así nos empoderamos.

Oye, si vas a caer víctima
Entonces cae víctima al Amor.

-MAJA

I Only Feel Safe When It's Toxic

Last night, you fell asleep with your fingers in my hair
and as your breaths deepened into dreamland,
your knuckles tightened to close around my strands,
two fists clutching me to you
as though you were a child scared of the dark
and i was the teddy bear that got you through it.
and it put such a tenderness in my heart to know
that even your subconscious mind
derived comfort from me
when it faced the unknown.

i like watching your focused face as you sleep
when i wake up before you,
observing the way your eyes dart back and forth
beneath the lids
as if your dream is hard to keep up with.
i like it because when your eyes flutter open,
a hazy smile immediately crawls across your lips
as my face is the first thing you see
upon reentering this dimension.

i was taught to look for solace in only myself
when i needed help.
i had to learn from a very young age

that no one in this world will support my weight
but me.
somehow, you make me forget
everything i've ever learned.
the child in me can't decide how to feel about that.

somedays when you hold me
i swear i can see you disappear
into the ghosts of every past lover that abused you.
and some nights my yoni tenses up, shuts down,
and i have to tell her that it's you,
and not any of the horrible men in my past,
that is touching me.

is it Santa Cruz that hardened you
and this island that keeps you soft?
or is it the other way around?
is it New York that froze my trust
and barricaded the cave around it
and California, the one that left
a flicker of warmth beneath?
and is it this land of no land
or your earth-cracked hand
that digs far enough to revive the flame
and coaxes the thawing of spring?

i want to know how one can tell
once wanting someone
starts to cross over into need.

is it when, instead of just looking forward to seeing you,
my body begins to crave your presence,
itches for you—
when i have trouble falling asleep on the nights
you're not there,
tossing and turning and drinking in your lingering scent
until i can find a position around a pillow
that mimics your warmth?
is it when,
after a lifetime of knowing
how to handle each of my emotional seasons on
my own,
my fingers instantly reach for the phone
when a storm descends?
is it when we're lying in bed, drifting off,
our mouths pressed so close together
we're depriving ourselves of oxygen,
breathing in each other's recycled air,
trading carbon dioxide back and forth until we
surrender?

this is the kind of love i've never understood.
this is the kind of love i've always been terrified of.

i spent my whole life learning the Art of
Non Attachment,
fighting with every muscle to break free
from the straitjacket of codependency.
it's taking so much effort to rewire my mind

to understand that wanting you,
that wanting to always be around you,
that wanting to teach my nomadic feet to stay in
one place
because of you,
that even
being willing
to give up certain aspects of my freedom
which i've carried on my shoulder as fiercely as my
self-sufficiency
in order to be with you —
does not have to be a bad thing.

see, you're the first person who told me they loved me
that i believed.
and still,
staring into your earnest eyes,
i am just barely learning how to receive it.

-Lavender Malin

Numero 5

Soñé que era agua
Y me derramaba entre tus labios.
Soñé que era sudor
descolgándome por tu pecho.
Soñé que era el tiempo
y me detenía cuando tu querías.
Soñé que era el viento
emanado por un suspiro tuyo.
Soñé que era fuego
calentando tu tentación.
Soñé que era voz
que por tu boca cantaba armoniosa.
Soñé que era tu amor y el mío,
el nuestro,
y me desperté amándote.
Y al amarte despertando
vi que a mi lado no estabas.
Que te difuminabas
como la estela de un cometa.
Que tu mirada café se alejaba
haciéndome un último guiño
de despedida.
Que tu olor volaba
como los pájaros,

que con el cielo acariciándolos
escapan al sur en invierno.
Y tus besos se fundían
con los rezagados rayos de sol.
que en el atardecer tratan de huir
de la llegada de la noche.
Aquí, entre los regalos que te brinda
la naturaleza
te amo en silencio.
Entre el recuerdo de lo que fue
y el despertar de lo que hoy es,
un sueño.
Te amé, te amo y te amaré
Aunque no pueda verte, ni oírte
ni besarte.
Amor bello, amor idealizado
amor futuro, eterno y pasado...

-Erick Szczurek

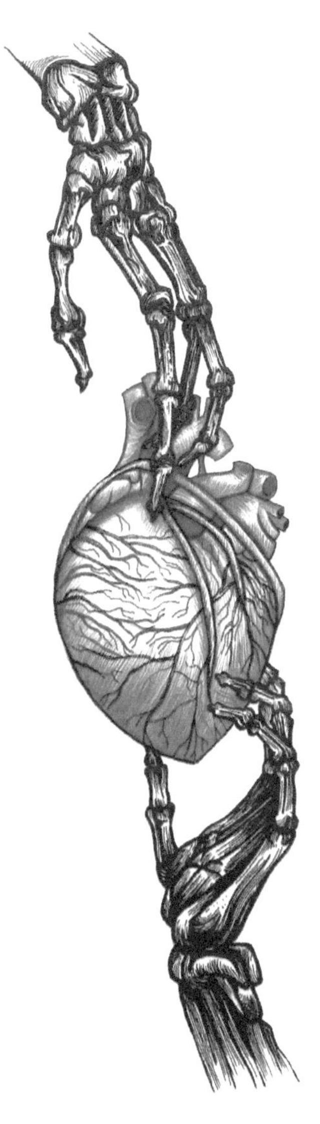

-Eddie Jelinet

Remplir Le Vide

J'ai un trou béant dans l'bide
Je voudrais tout lui donner sans brides,
À la dérive, juste pour vivre
Mais à quoi bon remplir le vide ?

Je voudrais pouvoir aimer, sans tout donner,
sans tout garder, sans tout gâcher,
tout gaspiller, pinailler pour éviter les frais,
rentrer dans les faits, savoir se placer,
que ça fasse de l'effet, m'empresser
sans peser, sans passé, sans presser
le citron à la passion, le sortilège à la potion,
thérapeutiques sont les poisons, rien n'est magique
devant la solution, le sale fric, la dissolution
j'abdique devant l'pavillon d'l'amour du risque et
je persiste devant la raison qui critique.
J'évite les bars, les bras de la mère qui s'agite,
elle m'imite, qui c'est qui pose les limites ?
Je lévite car c'est du vide qu'on hérite
et je sais même pas c'que je mérite, ça m'irrite,
au bout de l'appendice, l'affectivite vite.
De l'amour dans mon spleen sans espoir dans la rétine,
faut que je me donne, j'oublie les formes
car je suis hors norme

et Dieu sait que je m'y adonne, je m'époumone,
tu dèviens aphone et ça me bâillonne.
J'ai d'Hadès la faiblesse...

Si je suis teigneux c'est que le bas blesse
Si je suis taiseux c'est que je vois c'que God blesses
Et ce qui nous reste quand j'suis en manque d'adresse
Et qu'alors surgit la bête pour sacrifier ta tendresse.

Maudit j'erre, déter jusque dans ma chaire,
je me mets cher sans savoir c'qui m'est cher,
c'est pas demain que je pourrais dire «nous» frère.
Dans ma famille on est tous orphelins,
chez les vikings y a qu' des hordes de félins :
Les pères jalousent, volent et vendent
les enfants qu'ils craignent, vilipendent,
ils préfèrent t'ignorer, t'faire taire, ils profèrent
qu'on n'est que des erreurs d'hier.

Putain de sentiments d'exclusion,
toi qui est là comme depuis toujours,
qui s'immisce dans toutes mes fusions,
m'abandonneras-tu toi aussi un jour ?
On engendre des petits qu'on pourra pas
garder sans les emprisonner,
une engeance de type à te fracasser pour t'remercier.
Les êtres humains et leurs principes,
c'est attachant comme les petits chiens
mais les principes, ça va ça vient, suivant la faim.

Si tu fais la victime, si tu joues le til-gen,
c'est que tu as quelque chose à te reprocher.
Si tu fais le gros dur, que tu joues au méchant,
sûrement qu'on t'a trop amoché.
Si je suis misanthrope mon estime syncope
et devant l'œil du cyclope je te provoque.

J'ai plus peur de mourir, j'ai peur de revenir.

-el Malotonio

Ode

Ode to the dear friend from years ago
who was in hopeless, consuming, toxic love
with the sociopathic junkie girlfriend
of the avoidant alcoholic boy
whom i was hopelessly, toxically consumed with:

if we could do it over now,
maybe we could love ourselves louder.
maybe we could love ourselves hard enough
that we wouldn't have to fall into spirals
with those that could never fully see us.
maybe we could love ourselves fierce enough
to not get stuck in low self esteem loops with the ones
with dried hearts
that had no love left to give
because there was no love we were ready to receive.

all i really want to say is
wherever you are today,
i hope you're shining your own light so loud
so fierce and so hard
that your dazzling radiance is visible from acres and
acres away

and only those who are in reverence of its brilliance
and ready for its transformative, world-rattling force
shall dare to approach.

-Lavender Malin

30

Love to the Brown-Skin Girl

These words are for the moca, the coffee, the *café con leche*, the chocolate, the mixed yellow red and tan, for all the bronze and brown, for all the color-skin girls—
The ones who dreamt the dream, who believed in the "land of the free," who didn't question what it meant for a girl with colored skin;
The ones who woke up to poverty, winter with no heat, no chestnuts, no fire, no presents under any tree, who asked, does (white) Santa love me?
Who doe-eyed and trusting watched the cartoons and the endless fairytales and hoped for her very own prince charming, for her very own happy ending.
Who woke up to puberty, hating her body, trying to straighten her curves, trying to force her flesh into zero size jeans;
Who burned her scalp with relaxers and spent hours in front of the mirror, straight iron in hand, sweat on the brow, trying to flatten her kinks and curls into something pretty and "manageable."
These words for the color-skin girl who was told it's better to have super-sized breasts and a skull with no thoughts,
Who learned how to say please and thank you, how to speak the *correct* way,

Who learned to water down the coffee, to lower the
    voice, to take the spice out of the food…
Who averted the gaze, ignored the comments, looked
    down when they stared,
Who learned how to contort the mind, conceal the
    impulse, disguise the brain, mold the expression,
    master the muscles – how to construct the
    uncomplaining façade of conformity...

These words for the brown-skin girl who one day
meets Baldwin and Simone and Morrison and
Malcolm, who ask: *do you know who you really are?*
Where you come from? Where you got that skin?
What's written in your blood?
For the brown-skin girl who one day buckles under
    the weight of a billion burdensome un-truths,
Who one day knows she's being cheated, knows she's
    being used,
Who painstakingly tries to retrace the steps, unlearn
    the lie, re-learn the native song, reconnect the
    guarded soul…

These words are for the underpaid and overworked,
the sick and tired, for the fed-up color-skin girl–
Who's woken up to the rent unpaid, the bills overdo,
    the degree unfinished, the passion unclaimed, the
    potential still bound and shackled.
Who's been bought and sold, traded and debated in
    the endless business affair,

Who's punched the time clock, worked the 9-5,
    picked up the shifts, broken the back,
Who's put one foot in front of the other on the ever-
    spinning money wheel…

These words for the brown-skin girl who's found out
"freedom of choice" depends on the situation she's in…
Who's tried to beat the odds, to play the rigged
    game, to run twice as fast only to always be put
    in last place.
Who's tried to dull the aching head with whiskey and
    a doctor; tried to appease the wailing spirit with
    prayer and a melody;
Who's bore the brunt, taken the blows, assumed the
    guilt-ridden, perpetual blame,
Who's hidden the hurt away…

These words are for the color-skin girl who's trapped
in cement streets, in run-down, moldy-box buildings
in the domineering man's world…
Who yearns for something more,
Who dreams of seeds and the ocean and a wild breeze,
Who aches to know the pleasure of peace and ease,
Who wonders if she'll ever be free, if she'll ever get out,
    if they'll ever just let her live…just let her be…

Oh, beautiful, earthen-color-skin girl,
Oh precious daughter of the immigrant and the
    refugee, of the imprisoned and enslaved,

Oh daughter of space dust and the universe
     unfolding…
These words too little, too late to take away the scars,
to put down the needle,
to un-swallow the pills,
to right the wrong,
to take away the tears,
to loosen the load—

These words for you,
These words for me:

I love you.

I see you.

I too wear the ball and chain.

-A.Gallagher

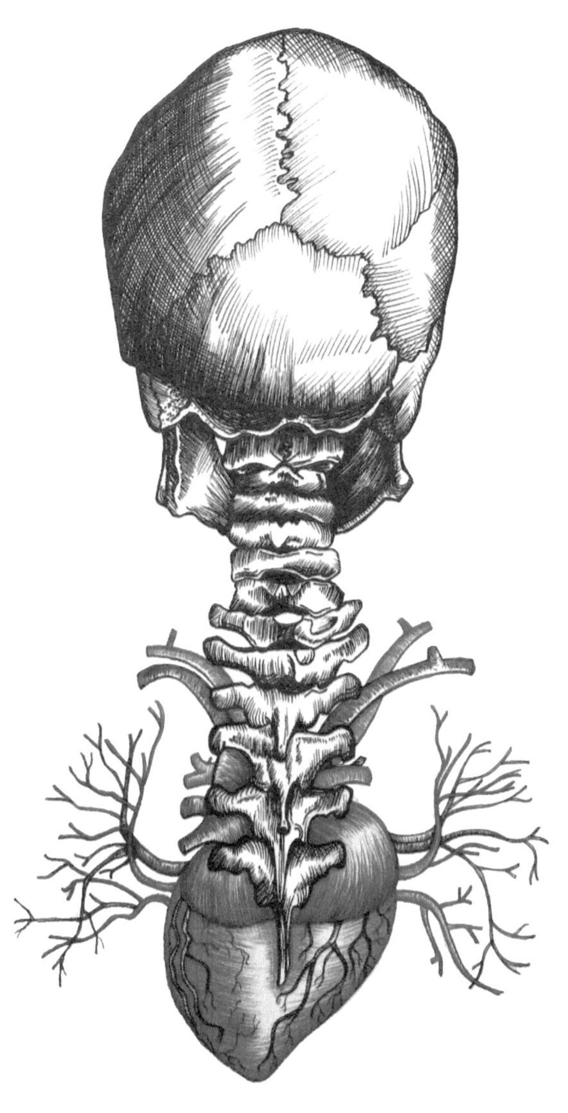

-Eddie Jelinet

C'est Un Beau et Triste Monde

Bon, déjà ça avait mal commencé.

Parce que je me suis réveillé avec une gueule de bois de dieu le père, de quoi tuer toute une promo d'étudiants et puis aussi parce qu'il n'y avait pas de café. La bonne vieille cuisine glauque à 6 heures du mat' m'ouvrait les bras. Ici, même les pots de yaourts sont des cendriers, un bordel incroyable, la table à manger ressemble à une ville pleine de buildings, de gratte-ciel et de monuments à 12 degrés 5. Un genre de mini New York déglingué faite de cendre et de tabac, de boîtes de pizzas, de canettes de bières et de bouteilles de vin plus ou moins vides. Je me suis servi un verre d'eau, fallait pas non plus déconner.

J'allais pointer à l'usine dans une heure, ce qui me laissait très exactement 4 minutes pour décoller vu que j'avais 56 minutes de trajet en bus à me coltiner. Dans mes calculs ça donnait ça. J'ai enfilé mes fringues collantes et puantes et je me suis tiré.

~

Tout le long du trajet j'essayais de lutter contre mon état en décomposition, je tentais de me redonner de l'énergie mentalement, en serrant les dents et les poings, pas franchement un succès, loin de là, à force de forcer, une furieuse envie de déféquer m'obligeât à serrer les fesses jusqu'au prochain arrêt.

Je me suis retrouvé sous l'abri bus tout contracté de l'intérieur, il faisait un temps de chien, je me suis confectionné une cigarette avec les restes de miettes de mon paquet de tabac et j'ai commencé à envisager le meilleur spot possible pour poser ma pêche de lendemain de cuite.

J'ai tourné autour de l'abri bus comme un toutou qui cherche son lampadaire, au fur et à mesure que j'avalais et que je recrachais la fumée, mon sphincter devenait de plus en plus intransigeant avec moi-même. J'ai donc été contraint de m'éloigner un peu de la route. Derrière moi, en contrebas, il y avait un petit bâtiment plein de fenêtres à rideaux tirés, sans doute les bureaux d'une entreprise quelconque. Je suis descendu devant la boîte en courant comme un canard, et je me suis prostré sous l'une des fenêtres, à l'endroit le plus discret pour y couler mon bronze. C'était épatant, sous la pluie diluvienne, sur un parterre de gazon anglais divisé en plates-bandes garnies de fleurs mignonnement jardinées, j'ai lâché mon cake jaunâtre en rugissant de plaisir, jamais mon corps ne m'avait si gracieusement remercié, mes fesses au vent sous la petite pluie du printemps, c'était un enchantement, une jouissance ineffable.

~

C'est donc le cœur léger que je me suis pointé à l'usine. Ici, à la chaîne, je triais des déchets, c'était mon rôle à moi dans ce monde si bien façonné. Toutes vos poubelles, tous vos détritus, toute votre merde, c'est moi qui la triait pour le recyclage. Autant dire un beau métier, très noble.

Prostré devant un tapis roulant gigantesque, on farfouillait parmi les couches de bébés usagées, les vieux jouets d'enfant cassés, les capotes, les emballages de bouffe périmée, les slips sales, les restes de dîner, les frites mal digérées, les épluchures de pommes de terre, les restes de gratin, les carcasses de poulet, parfois des chats morts, les ordures ménagères, les débris en tout genre, les résidus de vomi, les rognures, les raclures de tout, tout et puis tout le reste. Moi je devais localiser tous les bouts de bois qui défilaient sur le tapis pour les jeter dans la benne à bois, j'étais fort pour localiser le bois, le meilleur de toute l'usine. Sûr, c'est pas vraiment de la tarte, faut réussir à tenir le coup, beaucoup de gens dégueulent dans les bennes le premier jour. Moi, même en gueule de bois, je ne vomissais jamais.

~

Ici donc, bien à ma place, les yeux rivés sur le tapis, j'entre comme tous les jours dans l'état de coma nécessaire à la réalisation de ma tâche. Debout, les mains dans la merde, mes yeux roulent, se fixent sur le moindre morceau de bois, mes bras s'activent instantanément, je n'ai plus à me poser de questions, peu importe d'où viennent tous ces déchets, je rentre directement dans un état second, je deviens zombie, automate, insensible aux odeurs pestilentielles qui passent dans la salle de tri, je n'entends même plus les bruits sourds de l'usine en action, la ferraille qui claque et les gars qui gueulent, non, je suis dans une sorte de jeu vidéo, ma tête est un cockpit et mes bras sont des pinces programmées pour attraper le bois, dès que j'en vois, j'attrape je jette, j'attrape je jette, mon viseur est enclenché, bip bip, je localise, j'attrape je jette. Le temps qui passe ne fait plus partie de la réalité, plus aucune pensée, plus aucune introspection, plus d'état d'âme, plus rien ne se passe vraiment. Je ne suis plus en train d'évoluer dans ce monde-là. Non, entièrement débarrassé du dégoût, de la tristesse, de la lassitude, de la tête dans le cul et de la fatigue, les sens complètement déréglés comme dans un grand trip rimbaldien, je est un autre, plus léger, plus simple et plus pur. Moi je trie, la chaîne tourne. Elle tourne, tourne et tournera comme ça encore pendant des années, pendant des siècles jusqu'à ce que l'humanité s'effondre, des générations entières de galériens comme moi, de gamins qui n'ont jamais rien branlé à l'école seront là pour me succéder jusqu'à la fin des temps. En attendant je me frotte contre le tapis depuis des heures maintenant, le sexe à auteur de la machine, ma queue s'appuie contre le tapis à chaque fois que je me penche et je me rends compte au bout d'un moment que j'ai la trique. Tout en continuant de taffer, sans la moindre honte, je stimule mes organes génitaux sur cette chaîne répugnante, mon excitation prend des proportions anormalement grandes si bien que je finis littéralement par me branler à travers mon bleu de travail sur la machine. Je trie la merde en me branlant et je ne me pose aucune question, je ne pense à rien, surtout pas aux fantasmes obscènes et grotesques dont j'ai normalement besoin en intérieur pour m'exciter, je suis dans un état de plénitude absolue, juste moi et les résidus de la vie quotidienne de milliers de personnes, et c'est merveilleux. La chaîne s'arrête juste au moment où j'allais jouir. Je sors de la salle avec les autres ouvriers pour aller balayer les entrepôts de stockage de déchets, je me remets doucement de mes émotions et redeviens moi peu à peu, je dois avoir une drôle de gueule.

~

Les entrepôts sont gigantesques, partout à perte de vue des montagnes de papiers compactés en cube, des bouteilles en plastique formant des massifs de plus de 6 mètres de haut, des colonnes de pneus de bagnoles, des murs de cartons, des monticules de bois, de parpaings, de ferrailles, tout cela formant un paysage au relief hallucinant digne d'un film de science-fiction, genre post-apocalyptique. Je marche donc avec mes collègues au beau milieu de cette planète de débris, le vent souffle et s'engouffre dans les entrepôts faisant danser la poussière et les morceaux de papiers multicolores qui jonchent le sol sur des centaines de mètres carrés. J'observe un peu mes collègues qui commencent à s'affairer, armés des pelles et des balais, le masque recouvrant leur bouche et leur nez, la capuche rabaissée sur leur tête. Les lunettes de protection pleines de buée, ils se lancent dans la besogne sans broncher, sans se poser de questions, ils balayent comme une armée de robots un sol qui sera toujours sale. Dès qu'un coup de balai est passé, des centaines de bouts de polystyrène et autres petits déchets viennent se recoller instantanément au même endroit, une poussière immonde vole dans tous les sens. Au fond je pense que les patrons voudraient qu'on balaie l'air et le vent.

Je fais donc semblant de nettoyer le sol pendant quelques minutes, comme toujours je me dis qu'il faudrait que je prenne des photos de cet endroit incroyable ou alors que j'en fasse un tableau, un tableau fantastique rempli de couleurs, mais je ne sais pas dessiner. Le patron s'approche enfin pour me dire que la journée est finie, je jette ma pelle dans la réserve et je monte aux sanitaires me laver les mains et le visage, devant la glace je reprends un peu conscience de mon corps et de sa faiblesse, mes joues sont rouges, mes yeux piquent et mes cheveux collent, j'ai mal aux doigts mais cela ne fait rien. Comme souvent après le boulot, je pars seul de l'usine, je préfère être seul pour rentrer.

~

J'escalade une butte immense qui donne un point de vue imprenable sur les entrepôts et toute la zone industrielle, je m'assoie doucement pour ne pas effrayer les pigeons qui roucoulent toujours ici et qui picorent n'importe quoi. Alors en respirant calmement l'air souillé qui m'entoure, je m'adonne à mon passe-temps favori. Je sors de ma poche des poignées de riz cru que je lance aux oiseaux, le riz cru à cette particularité qu'il est indigeste surtout pour les petits estomacs, j'attends ensuite silencieusement que la magie opère. J'observe presque avec tendresse ces petites bestioles ridicules et sous évoluées, prêtes à avaler tout ce qu'on leur donne, dernières sur l'échelle des espèces volatiles, laides et stupides, éboueurs des villes mais pourtant capables de voler et de tracer dans le ciel des dessins de liberté. C'est alors que commence le ballet macabre. Tandis qu'il arrive des pigeons de partout, ceux qui se sont bien rassasiés de mon riz repartent nerveusement au-dessus des entrepôts de l'usine et explosent en plein vol comme des bombes de plumes grises, roucoulant une dernière fois sur cette terre pleine de beauté et de tristesse. Je regarde d'abord le spectacle dans son ensemble, le ciel rose, le soleil qui décline et tous ces pigeons qui volent et qui explosent comme s'il s'agissait d'un grand feu d'artifices vivant, puis je m'attarde sur certains d'entre eux, celui qui avait une tache sur le cou par exemple, ou celui qui boitait un peu et je les suis du regard du décollage jusqu'à l'explosion, quand leurs plumes, leurs tripes et leurs boyaux se répandent partout dans la zone industrielle. J'aime ce moment, j'ai l'impression qu'il s'inscrit dans la logique des choses, qu'il fait partie d'un grand tout.

~

Dans le bus, sur le trajet du retour, je pense en souriant à mon patron qui m'a encore dit que je faisais du bon boulot et je me dis que ce monde est affreusement comique, tu peux brasser du caca tous les jours, si quelqu'un te dit que tu es doué pour ça, tu finiras toujours par être flatté et fier de toi. Alors j'essaie de ne pas pleurer et de ne surtout pas penser à l'avenir.

Quand j'arrive chez moi, je passe par la cuisine qui n'a pas changé mais qui me semble moins sale que ce matin, je trouve mon colocataire tremblant dans un fauteuil du salon, en pleine descente de je ne sais quelle drogue forte, incapable de lever la tête ou d'articuler un mot, il sent ma présence parce que je pue, il s'efforce de se redresser un peu, je me dirige vers ma chambre sans faire attention à lui et alors il me demande tant bien que mal comme tous les jours : « ça a été le boulot ? »

Et moi je me rends compte qu'il ne me reste plus que quelques heures avant de tout recommencer.

-*Grégoire Parville*

<h1 style="text-align:center"><s>Censured</s></h1>

I want to crawl out of my body
I want to cut my stomach open from the inside,
Stick one leg out
And then the other
And be free of the flesh that weighs me down,
Spit on the judgment that mills in my cranium,
Crack my skull with my screams.

I want to slip out, skinny and slimy,
Ready for a new world that is cool,
As a cucumber,
Cool
As juicy melon dripping down my chin on a hot
summer day.

I want to punch my nose,
Make it bleed,
Watch it bleed,
Bleed,
And bleed onto the carcass I have left behind,
Onto the layers of jelly that line my skin,
The shell I don't want,
The cellophane that clings to my fat.

"You look like a painting," I've been told.
"A painting or a fresco, or a marble statue."
"Something like that."

Well how about de Kooning?
Oil, and splatter, and grotesque angry shapes -
That's what's left of me now.

I'll pick my teeth with my own bones,
Write alabaster bitch on the walls,
Rip my breasts out with my bare hands,
Shake the envelope that's left until I finally decide
It's time
To crawl back in
Stick one leg in
And then the other
And bite my tongue so I don't cry.

-Tamara Sevunts

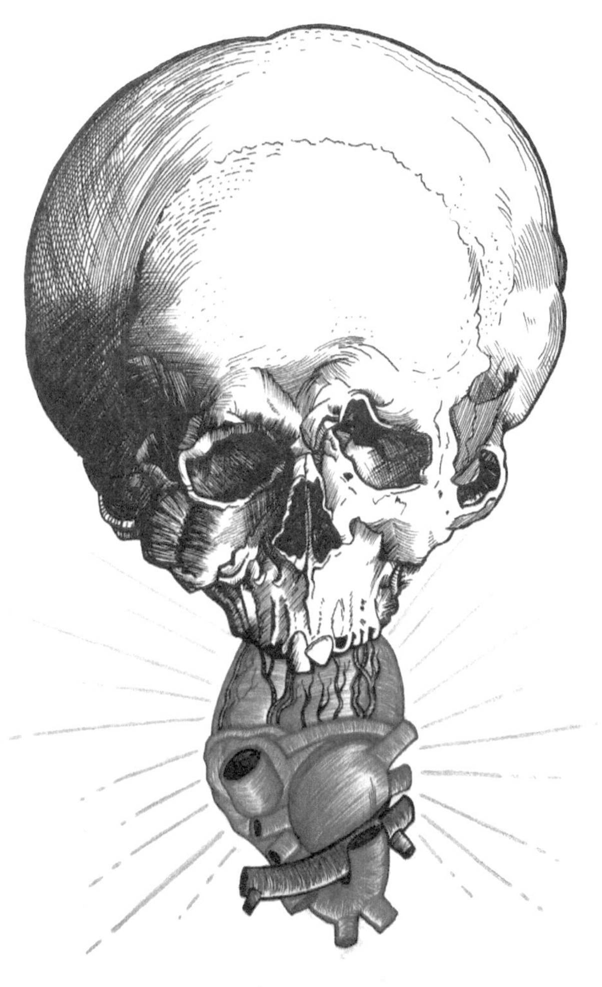

-Eddie Jelinet

Numero 7

Blanca Soledad regalada,
de miradas esquivas que nada observan,
de polvo detenida,
tu semblante contemplan.

Consecuente la ruta caminada,
las mentiras que se apartan,
mantienes el hálito de vida
y los fantasmas te abandonan.

De tu lengua palabra silenciada,
vacías tus manos gesticulan,
copa de ira desierta, agotada,
las fatigas no te encuentran.

Pensamiento de madera astillada,
volar cielos que en tus sueños abundan,
no verte en tu destino consumida,
las notas armónicas emocionan.

La llama de tu alma encendida
cegando a los que engañan,
mano de hierro contenida
golpeando susurros que condenan.

En galaxias fuiste engendrada,
átomos de magia te adornan,
verdades de pureza manifestada,
como las ramas de zarza se enredan.

Y de esta blanca soledad regalada
infitas glorias se conservan,
impresas en eterna memoria congelada
que como tifones a los idiotas devastan.

Vulgar la falacia furcia disfrazada,
de las lombrices los gallos se alimentan,
la cascada de la noche es derramada
y sus demonios con ella fornican.

Al amanecer le canta el sol a su amada,
dorados rayos como trompas entonan
la melodía por los vivos deseada,
el himno de alegría todos cantan.

Tela compleja con maestría hilada,
aguas en mares navegan,
tu verdad, la mía, por todos colmada
espejos del cosmos reflejan.

-Erick Szczurek

La Colère Qui Fuse

La colère qui fuse, les problèmes somatisent,
la galère qu'infuse, je m'assomme à la tise,
t'étonne pas qu'j'abuse quand les sots m'attisent,
si tu me prends pour une buse mon assaut dératise.

C'est à ce monde de merde qu'il faut survivre.
Qu'ils me fuient ou qu'ils me suivent,
plus je suis moi même, plus ils me craignent,
'cause I wear my own despair.

Soutenir mon regard est devenu oppressant ;
ils s'enfuient tous en balbutiant
parce qu'en m'regardant, s'rappellent
que souvent, les mots sont des faux semblants.

Pour remplir le temps, moi j'entends le vent ;
le vent venir le vent tourner, le vent partir le vent passer,
le ventriloque et le vantard, le vendu, la vendetta,
l'avide et le vandale, le ventre vide le vent détale.

T'es tellement en manque de fiction
qu'il faut que je parabole et qu'je me prostitue.
Je suis tellement en manque d'affection
qu'en réalité je te viole quand ma prose te tue.

Ils n'arrêtent pas de se plaindre, de geindre et de
se morfondre,
ils ne savent que craindre et attendre la fin du monde.
Ils ne savent pas quoi faire que de raconter tout ce
qu'ils ne feront jamais R.
Ils font R pépère, moi j'erre dans l'terter.

Ici bas le niveau est bas, à ras de terre.
C'est facile de penser qu'on peut rien n'y faire,
dire qu'on sauvera la terre en étant solidaire
pour sauver sa carrière et se croire salutaire.

La colère qui fuse, les problèmes somatisent,
la galère qu'infuse, je m'assomme à la tise,
t'étonne pas qu'j'abuse quand les sots m'attisent,
si tu me prends pour une buse mon assaut dératise.

D'abord les gens contents ça me saoule,
z'arrêtent pas d'se plaindre c'est lourd.
Tu sais que l'argent comptant rend sourd,
savent pas écouter sans faire la morale et des
grands discours.

On se monte des histoires, on fait tout pour y croire,
surtout ne pas voir, ne pas laisser voir nos déboires.
Les belles paroles au parloir, ils voudraient te voir les
boire, et y pourvoir, juste pour voir...

Et on oublie la trajectoire,
c'est l'ironie du désespoir :
réussir en somme à aimer ses débris
même si personne ne nous a appris.

Alors on délivre la rage dans la grande cage
et y'a pas que sur la page qu'on reste sauvage.
Dans c'monde du père du-per
si t'es pas en colère, c'est toi qu'est pas clair.

-el Malotonio

*"Those Who Think They Are Above Animals
Live Worse Than Animals"*
–Don Juan, <u>A Separate Reality</u>

I have a confession to make.
Disguised in proper manners and a controlled exterior,
I am actually something of a raging bitch.

I try to keep it under control.
I regularly prescribe myself yoga and meditation and
Try to focus on breathing, just breathing…but
I have to admit:
When I walk down the street,
My skin twitches at the sight of all the
pornographic publicity,
My nose burns from the blocked-in acidity,
My eyes are red and itchy and I'm raging. I'm raging!

Whose machines are ripping down these trees?
Who's responsible for the pavement below my feet?
You have brought out the bitch in me.

Too long I have been trained to trade my instinct for
Branded, plastic clothing and vapid entertainment;
Trained to acquiesce and excuse until finally beaten
into complicity

To cut away the limbs, dig up the roots, say
yes drug me! Yes use me!
In this rancid wasteland of just do it! Make it feel
good! Make it look good!
"Paint your face," they tell me.
"Muzzle your lips," they say.
"Now be a good girl, come over here and sit."

But I'm not a good girl; I'm what they call "a bitch."
I have no interest in being good or goods or an
obedient participant.
Too long I have forgotten I am the kin of wild wolves!
Who thick skinned, clear-eyed and howling
Made men tremble, made men stop and listen.

So when the patriarchal hand, blood-stained with
morale and religion,
Reaches for me or for my children
I'll bite back, I'll break flesh, I'll let my teeth sink in.
And maybe you'll call me beastly, ugly, or unladylike
But at least I can walk with my head held high.
And if I am expected to be a "proper woman:"
Beauty primped and pimped, docile, subservient
and puppy-eyed,
Well my confession is I would rather be a bitch.

-A.Gallagher

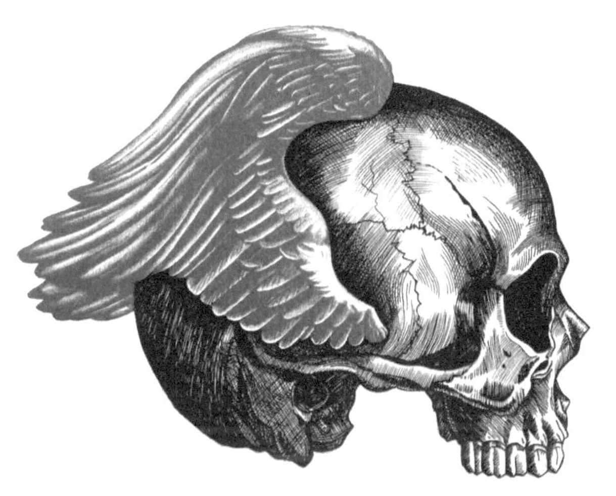

-Eddie Jelinet

Worth

The vibration from the subway busker's violin rattles the cup of coffee I shouldn't be drinking, clutched in between my hands like an altar candle. I can feel the vibration as it crawls from the styrofoam sides to the surface of my skin, then pulsates into my bones, up the tendons of my arms, through my spine. My body is an echo chamber.

In this underground tunnel, dozens of commuters flurry past in hoards, exhausted 9-5ers racing home during rush hour. But leaning against a sturdy yellow pillar with my eyes closed, the violinist's soft jazz dimension washing over me like a cooling breeze by the sea, I can't see nor hear any of them. There is only the stillness, the calm, the woven auditory tapestry of the lazy drawl of *Tenderly* crooning from this instrument, freezing me in an embrace, in this time out of time. I have been here, paused and free, enraptured in the feeling that this childhood favorite standard invokes in me, for a decade. A moment. An eternity.

The violin croons the song to a gentle resolution. I should open my eyes, break free from this separate reality, and continue on my way home. I've got things to do, I think, or so my brain likes to tell me. But before I decide to remove myself from this orchestra of an ocean, the busker strikes up his wand again. *Claire de Lune* reels me back into the timeless vortex. It's a song I've often listened to in my room in meditation, in my ears on the train, walking through the hypomanic streets of Manhattan, transmuting chaos to connection. A song that has always brought me back home. A song that once called across the desert to me, when I was lost deep within a bad acid trip, biking in endless circles around and around Black Rock City, spiraling into the wild underworld of my loneliness. The hymn had retrieved me; it trickled into my eardrums like a soothing stream in the dry dust, and played out to me from an art installation miles away, so far I shouldn't have been able to hear it. I had paused, saved from my never-ending bike loops, and then drew nearer and nearer, like a wayward moth coming back to the light, to the beckoning piano that had a message only for me. *Claire de Lune* was a prayer, a beacon that radiated the words: *You are not alone. You are not alone. You are not alone.*

The busker's strings sing these words to me now, to comfort me in this time out of time, to take my hand and soothe me as I prepare to step out of this womb and re-emerge into the rest of the world: *You are not alone. You are not alone. You are never alone.*

And though there are a thousand blurs of energy passing by, and though the rush of arriving trains above my head rattles my entire body, and though my hips are still clenched with the weight of the last middle-aged man that touched me a mere twenty minutes ago- there is no one, no one, no one here but me, the violin, the magician wielding it, and the universe holding me, carrying me, kissing me through the oars of Debussy.

It is only a million light years later, after I breach the surface, give the busker some cash and a solidarity smile, and surrender to the stream of busybodies churning toward the L train, that my consciousness reunites with the tight pain in my pussy.

~

There are the ones who come to you because they have an elaborate fantasy to fulfill– a fantasy they are too afraid to ask of their partners, their wives, or their one-night stands. A fantasy they perceive others wouldn't understand. A request they're too embarrassed or ashamed of to ask anyone but the sex worker.

There are the basic submissives, the ones who want to be whipped, spit on, slapped, face-sat. There are the insecure, misogynistic, and slightly sociopathic dommes, the men who want to assert their power and enact upon their hidden, primal rape desires. There are the ones who want to be humiliated, who want you to ridicule them for how small their dicks are as you fuck them, the ones who call you mommy and want you to scold them for being a bad little boy. There are the ones who want you to wear nothing but knee-high stockings and pretend you're an innocent, corruptible young schoolgirl, who calls them "Sir" and gasps in surprise as they enter you.

Then, there are the men who simply want to be held, touched, the ones who want to stare deep into your eyes and stroke your face slow and make believe you two are in love. There are the ones that are so lonely and socially awkward it is clear that they would not have the nerve to talk to a woman, let alone be intimate with her, any other way. There are the ones that simply want someone to talk to. There are the ones that wouldn't have the time, energy or desire to put in the effort required toward meeting a sexual partner in non-transactional ways. There are the ones who believe humans are meant to be polyamorous, while their libido-lacking wives do not.

And then, there are the ones that believe that sex has the potential to simply be a freeing, cathartic activity – that it can be pure, light, and fun – and have no qualms whether they receive it from a partner, from a consenting adult at a bar, or by paying for it. These are the men that have always been my favorite clients.

Jeremy is one such client. An unabashed sex freak, it is clear from the moment he walks through the door of the Midtown massage parlor (or HJP– "Hand Job Palace"– as a friend who used to work here not-so-affectionately likes to call it) that he is simply here to have some fun with the nice wad of funds burning a hole in his pocket. It's refreshing, these rare clients who aren't walking in with a suitcase full of trauma that they unceremoniously dump on you as soon as their clothes hit the chair– trauma they haven't even begun to bring their awareness to. (Trauma that this line of work will do nothing to help heal.)

He's tall, over six feet, slender, shaggy blonde hair. Not hideous. Mid 40s. He's wearing a Monkees T-shirt; we briefly discuss our favorite 60s bands as I pour him a glass of water and he relieves himself of his shin-high Doc Martens and jeans. Looks kind of silly in a middle-aged teenage boy sort of way, sitting there on the edge of the bed in just a band shirt, red boxers and tall white socks, long legs swinging.

We've exhausted our mutual appreciation list of The Zombies, Turtles, Byrds, Doors and Hendrix. He inquires how old I am (they always do) and expresses his surprise that I have a taste in old music for twenty-five (as they always do), then grumbles something about how shitty his day at work was (again, sticking to the formula).

"What do you have in mind for tonight's session?" I ask him with a warm smile, as I slip off my pink silk robe (Victoria's Secret, but it was a $30 score at a vintage thrift shop in Williamsburg. Thank fucking God, because I wouldn't have thrown my hard-earned dollars at Victoria Secret's overpriced bullshit otherwise). He takes in my black lace bra and panties with a slightly gaped open mouth, eyes getting trapped down the midpoint of my cleavage.

"Well, actually…" Clearing his throat, he reaches into his bag and pulls out a large white vibrator. "You ever like playing with toys? I want to make you come as much as possible."

"Mm. I'm into it." I unclasp my bra and set it on the windowsill, allowing him to soak in my breasts. His eyes, as clients' always do, lingers on my chest tattoo. I can tell he's curious but also too eager and horny to ask about it. I'm glad – it's a long story and I have no desire to attempt the carefully gift-wrapped words needed to give a short reply.

He reaches for his jeans, fumbles around for his wallet.

"Just so you know, since this is your first time with me," I say carefully, "I know every girl here does it differently, but it's $100 extra from the massage rate if you want to touch me, and $160 if you want to use your tongue."

His face tightens a bit, and he pauses in his wallet search. "Really? Touching isn't included?" His eyes scan my body again, as if considering whether my perky breasts are still worth it. "That's kind of a rip off, don't you think?"

Ah yes. He's one of the cheapskate complainers. We get a lot of those. Many of these men think they should be entitled to touching us, eating us, fucking us for under $300. The basic rate for a massage + hand job is $220; the house gets 90 of that, while I get 130. Allowing the men to touch you/finger you is optional, along with any other extras (i.e. giving or receiving oral, fucking, anal, etc). Each girl decides if she wants to allow extras, and sets her price for them. There ain't no fucking way a slimy old fucker gets to touch me for less than 200.

We market by offering tantric massage on the hidden online ads, or "FBSM"- full body sensual massage, hand job implied within those parameters. But we can't outwardly mention any other sexual acts through the ads because that's what the cops are after. Advertising "full service" is a screaming invitation for an undercover agent to try to book a session with you and worm his way into the apartment.

Every girl at this collective is different, and while almost all of the girls charge extra for mutual touching, some charge only 50 or 60 over the base massage rate, while one girl even does all extras for free, though the rest of us feel that's in bad taste– she makes it harder for us to charge for the same services. She also happens to be the only girl in the collective who shit-talks and tears down her fellow sex workers and is just generally an all-around bitch.

Sizing up this overgrown teenager in HJP's dingy Victorian queen poster bed, I choose my words with care. Every cheapskate needs a slightly different response to assuage his doubts and remind him this is what he wants. "I know what I'm worth, love," I say with a deep sultry tone, sliding my left leg out so that he can see the crease of my pussy against my black lace panties. His eyes fall on the few gentle wisps of pubic hair crawling out. I can tell he's into it by the way his lips part slightly. "I can keep my underwear on if you like and only take care of you, or we can have some *real* fun together."

His gaze on my crotch is charged and feverish. The weight of his arousal is palpable. A tongue darts out from the opening in his mouth and swipes across his lower lip, so offhand it seems unintentional. His hands resume their search for his wallet. "I want to taste you," he says in a voice unable to contain his excitement, counting out $380 onto the table.

I smile and keep direct eye contact as I ever so slowly pull down my lacy bottoms. His lower lip drops slightly as he stares.

At first, he's giddy and anxious as I lay him down and begin to weave my hands across his back, not unlike an inexperienced schoolboy covering further bases for the first time with a girl he deems is out of his league: slow, trembling, hesitant, face transfixed in awe at the fact that he even gets to be in this situation. As I knead with my chest and waist pressed into his back, his fingers reach behind him to graze my ankles, crawl up my legs, rest timidly on my ass. It doesn't take him long to pick up more gusto, grabbing me with hungrier hands before moving off his back, flipping me over and sliding his fingers inside me.

A variety of body parts and tools are used: fingers, two different dildos he's brought, and finally, his tongue. It's a pleasant surprise to find he actually knows how to effectively work a vagina with the latter; most clients don't. I come once, twice, three times. He grins and gasps alongside my moans, ever so often mentioning how hot it is to hear me react, echoing the fairly common rhetoric of "I love giving you pleasure, baby." I'd be lying if I said I wasn't having fun.

I decided at the very beginning of my escorting career that there's no point or need to limit pleasure from myself while I'm working. Orgasms are one of my favorite perks of the job. Some girls don't like to come with clients; they feel it's too intimate. But for me, if you're touching me I sure as hell want to be getting more out of it than just the money. Long gone are the days where I'm content with orgasmless sex. It doesn't happen every time, of course, but my years of sleeping with incompetent (and uncaring) men have taught me how to make my pussy come on its own no matter how well the tongue or fingers are doing with it. (Kegel-orgasm manipulation doesn't work quite so well with penetration, however.)

Some girls also don't mind kissing clients, but swapping saliva has always felt far more intimate to me than coming. The head is where our crown and third eye chakras are; the head is home to the center of our energetic field, our personality, our thoughts, our soul. When I kiss someone, I feel the core of who they are more than I do from engaging with any other part of the body. That is something I keep for my personal life alone.

We're nearing the end of the hour when Jeremy finishes taking advantage of my ability to have an incredible amount of orgasms within a short window. When it's his turn, he comes quickly, easily, releasing just after I've barely started working on him. The easy finishers are the best clients; my wrists are endlessly grateful for them.

Jeremy lets out a breathless "Wow!" when he's done, says it again when he cleans himself up. He continues to repeat the word with gusto as he gets dressed. Donned back in his display of middle-aged punk nostalgia, he shakes his head and grins at me with that same concoction of dorky childishness. "Wow. Thanks a lot! You're amazing, you are! Really incredible. This was so great."

"It was. I had a lot of fun," I say, with a little more authenticity than the phrase usually holds. His genuine enthusiasm is hard to dislike.

"When are you available next? I need to make you come so many more times. I've got more fun helpers at home I'd love to bring." He gestures toward the vibrators.

We schedule a session for next week. As I slip on my pink robe and lead him to the door, I mention the possibility of full service for next time (for an additional $240). I'm not open to having sex with every client; usually it's only the ones I feel comfortable with and can tell that I would enjoy, or at least, tolerate it. He practically squirms with excitement at the suggestion.

"You're such a rocket, sweetheart!" he gushes at the door, kissing me on the cheek. "Thanks so much, wow. I absolutely cannot *wait* to see you Wednesday!" I chuckle a bit as he practically skips into the building's first floor hallway.

I never see Jeremy again. On Monday night, I text him to confirm our upcoming appointment. He responds with the following:

Hey Ruby! Had such an amazing time with you last week and loved LOVED helping you orgasm(s)! Unfortunately, I have to cancel Wednesday. Owing you complete honesty, the costs of extras with you are a bit exorbitant for a massage girl's services; they're more in line with full service escort rates. Not complaining! You're such a gem and a cool and amazing woman. Just can't do those prices for what you're offering. Maybe in the future, if you lower your rates to amounts that more equate the services rendered.

I can't say I'm too surprised, or even that annoyed. After working at Hand Job Palace for eight months, and in sex work in general for over a year, I'm used to it by now. FBSM is seen as the lower-class end of prostitution. A majority of the clientele perceives hand-job masseuses as the lowest tier of the sex work hierarchy, far below dominatrices, strippers and, particularly, escorts belonging to agencies. They often expect our rates to match that judgment.

Yes, there are higher-respected platforms of hooking that I've desired to work through. I remember reading *The Intimate Adventures of a London Call Girl* when I was a teenager and fantasizing about working for an escort agency. But New York is London's trashier cousin, and the fancy agencies here that pay escorts quite a lot require the individual to be in with an elite crowd to find them. And even then, they are upfront about their need for their girls to be super skinny, have no tattoos, and look like photoshopped images on magazine covers. I once reached out to an agency whose information I acquired from a coworker, but they stopped responding after I sent over photos, seeing as I'm covered in body art, and my body type is far closer to Marilyn Monroe than Reese Witherspoon.

My opinion? Sex work is sex work. All hookers, escorts, exotic dancers and employees in the sex trade are equal and should be regarded– and paid– as such, at *whatever* high amount the goddess deems her own body to be valued. And when a woman offers up her body as a commodity, it should be treated as the fucking high-class, top-shelf, dazzling diamond-and-gold value that it is, no matter what venue out of which she chooses to advertise it.

To Middle-aged Teenage Boy, I write back the simple statement:

My rates mirror the level of value & respect I have for myself, and for the services I provide. If you are seeking cheaper rates for the same services, I suggest you find a woman who values her body and services below what she's worth. Have a great week.

But I do not blame him. He is a byproduct of his environment, of a disgusting pyramid-scheme system that encourages its slaves to find intimacy in methods that are as quick, easy, and cheap as humanely possible. It is from the system itself that this injustice and corruption stems from. And I, too, am a byproduct of a system which has forced me to work shitty, dignity-slaughtering, half-penny-paying jobs all my life, until I found the one thing I can sell that is worth something half-valued in this society, the one thing that is finally even worth a decent amount of money and does not break my body and mind down for hours-on-end like bartending and nannying did: my body itself.

No, I do not blame Jeremy. I blame the system that steeped its beliefs into him, the silent beast that programmed him all his life to place so little value, monetary or otherwise, toward a woman, her body or the gifts she can provide. Jeremy's attitude, like so many men that come to HJP, is a direct, successful result of capitalism's ruthless machine: a robotic mind and a numbed-down emotional center, scheming and calculating to get the most gain from the fewest amount of dollars, time and effort spent after slaving away and making tons of money for someone higher on the chain than himself.

And who am I to *not* capitalize on his output, and the output of many men like him, for the sake of my own survival and prevailment against the same machine?

-Roe Taylor

Petites Pensées Pesantes

Le 22 octobre
Je souffre de diarrhée
J'ai bu trop de thé Ultra Slim
Recette chinoise secrète
Passée de millénaire en centenaire
À l'industrie capitaliste américaine
(Le train roule et il me reste huit stations avant la
toilette)
Il y a deux jours, je pesais
133 livres— 3 livres se sont évaporées du jour au
lendemain
Maintenant, je pèse 136.4 livres
Sûrement les hormones
C'est ça, les hormones !
Ce qui me rend femme, ce qui
m'empêche d'être femme parfaite dans le regard
de l'industrie capitaliste américaine
Ça ne change rien au fait
qu'avec un peu de succès
Je suis renouvelée dans mon avarice,
alléchée par des coussins, des rideaux
Je veux adoucir la lumière dans ma chambre
Créer mon propre clair-obscur
Me poser comme une muse classique—

ronde, blanche, douce,
molle, aussi
136.4 livres de porcelaine—
chinoise, pourquoi pas ?

Le 1er avril
Poisson d'avril :
Ma balance me montre 126.2 livres
Deux livres de plus que le mois dernier
On me demande un poème matinal
Et me voilà tout d'un coup coincée
Comme mon poids qui résiste
À s'alléger

Peut-être si je laisse les mots s'écouler de mes
paupières enflées
Si je les vomi de ma gueule de bois
Si je les laisse marcher—
Une armée de fourmis noires qui s'échappe de mes
pores, de mon nez,
Peut-être pourrai-je me débarrasser de
Ces quelques livres qui résistent encore et toujours
à ces thés,
Ces sueurs, ces attentes, ces efforts à moitié réalisés
Et je réalise en riant :
C'est mon cœur qui pèse autant ce matin
C'est à mon cœur de perdre du poids
Espèce d'enfoiré

-Tamara Sevunts

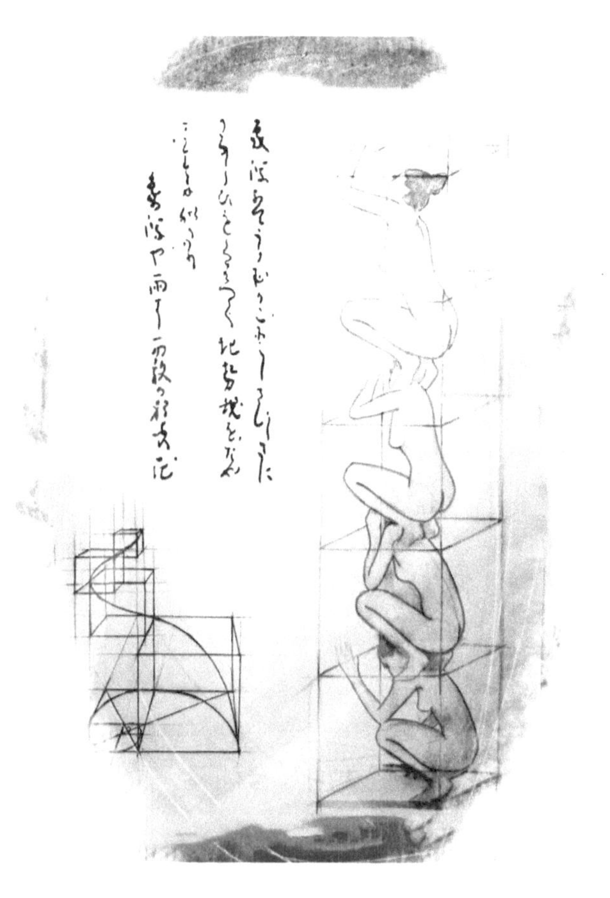

-Rebecca Landi

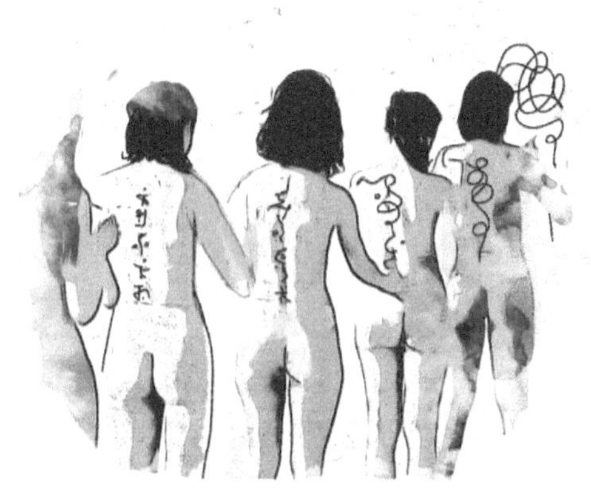

$$\sum \vec{F} = 0$$

$$\sum \vec{F} = m\vec{a}$$

$$\vec{F}_{1,2} = -\vec{F}_{2,1}$$

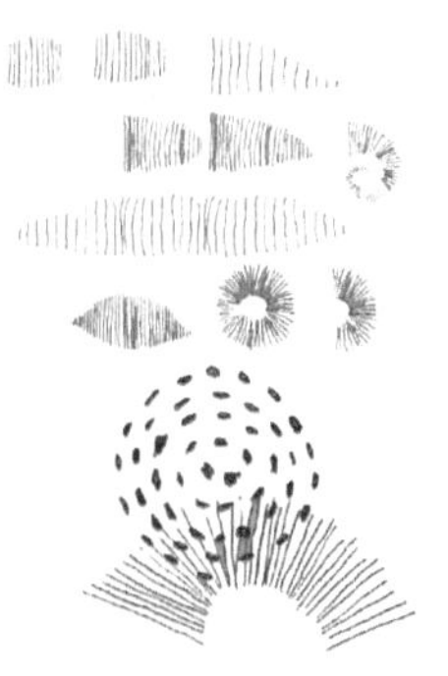

-Rebecca Landi

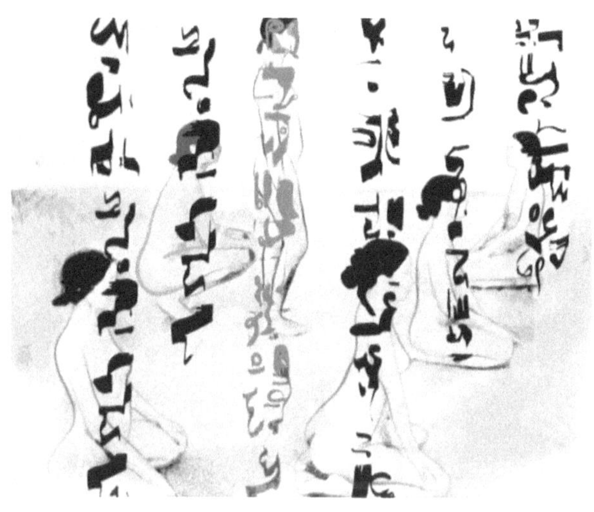

-Rebecca Landi

-Rebecca Landi

Some Things I Think About
When I Think of Love

I am in the darkness locked in a cupboard under the stairway. I am in kindergarten, and the nuns have put me on punishment once again. I cannot remember exactly why, but it has something to do with using my left hand, or for not learning, or for not meeting some expectation. I stand behind the locked door and cry and pray please, please, I'm sorry, please, please, god, help me.

As a child I am too loud, too unruly, too dramatic. My laugh is slightly savage, the pitch a bit too maniacal. My hair is too big and my expression too dreamy, my manner too aloof. Shock treatments-various punishments from leather-belted beatings to solitary confinement, from shouts to stern disapproving lectures are used to teach me a few things, teach me about reality. All the corrections and manhandling and stings done for my good, by people who say they love me…

I grow up a loner, a good pretender, an intelligent observer, a student of contexts, and I start to notice a few things about this thing called "Love," about "I Love you" and its meaning…

Like how "I love you" can be a gift or a

weapon, it just depends on how it's said, how it's given. Or how Love can give you some of what you need, but not necessarily what you really hoped for or wanted. I notice that "I love you" can be a kind of exchange: it can put food on the table, provide a warm bed to sleep in and clothes to wear in return for servile gratitude and a body that won't complain. I see how, sometimes, Love seems like a contractual agreement… That no matter how many times people promise the contrary, Love seems to always have demands, always have conditions.

I notice how people will say that you don't know how to love, or that you're too angry, or that you're toxic because you're set to explode. Or they'll say, "that one just wasn't The One…You just have to move on, try again." Or they'll say, "that wasn't love, that was dependency. Maybe *you* are attracting the *wrong* person…Love is more feel-good, more passion and happy-endings…"

I start to notice how all the songs and slogans say "all you need is love." But when you're hungry or when you can't pay the bills, or when you're sick and tired; when you live above the crazy, fascist neighbor, in a cement block, in a moldy house or in your car, Love doesn't really seem to cut it.

I notice how people will tell you: "you have to love yourself before anyone will love you." So maybe you're just not loving yourself *enough* or in the *best* way…? Maybe you need a prescription from the psychiatrist or a bit more self-help...? But, then again, I notice it's hard to "love yourself" when you're not exactly "all right." When you have baggage, or when you've been isolated, secluded, beaten, or somehow betrayed.

So I get to thinking and considering... Maybe I don't really know anything about Love. Or maybe Love is different than what I've known Love to be. Maybe everything depends on who's doing the loving. Or maybe, in this world, the one I've lived in, Love is just not enough to keep a person sane.

-A.Gallagher

Cherimoya

"I've been having nightmares every night," Bernadette told Dr. Halon.

"What about?"

"Dying. Every dream's the same."

Bernadette stood up from her cat-scratched leather Chesterfield and began to pace, grasping her blunt fringe bangs in one hand like strands of burnt-blackened straw between her fingertips, and in the other hand clutching a phone glued to her ear. Her kohl-lined eyes were closed as she spoke as if she were trying to steady her voice by visualizing her words: picturing each sentence like a subtitle underlining a film or like the animated letters bouncing on a karaoke screen. Trying to quell the smell of the fresh kitty shit newly defecated in the lavender-corn litter box from permeating her senses. She was unable to suppress her laughter. Unable to breathe.

"Have you been eating spicy foods before bedtime?" Dr. Halon asked, disregarding her laughter.

He doesn't hear me, Bernadette thought to herself. "No, I don't eat spicy food. I don't have a tolerance for it."

"Do you drink before bed?" he asked her.

"Sometimes," she said. *Usually*, she thought.

"Well, that might explain it. A glass of wine, or two, is acceptable however give yourself some time to enjoy. Probably best to stop a few hours before turning in," Dr. Halon prescribed.

"I've tried that."

"Have you tried taking a break then?"

"From what?" she asked.

"Drinking."

Bernadette hung up the phone and opened the refrigerator to retrieve a fresh bottle of chilled vodka. She placed it on the tile-patterned bar which separated the living space from the kitchen in her box of a studio. She sighed, feeling the way she did every morning when she reached across her bed to find that it was empty. She'd slide her fingers up and down the sheets, then in between her legs, searching for something, someone, who wasn't there anymore—his warmth, his soul, his heart. Missing as usual.

Seizing a brush from on top of the microwave, Bernadette began to sweep through her thick black hair, split ends and broken strands falling onto the kitchen floor. Then with shaking hands, she twisted the cap off the bottle and tipped the mouth of it down her throat. A cold liquid glow swam down her gullet, and she could breathe again.

"Hello," Bernadette said to herself. She buckled on her fanny pack and stuffed it with a satiated flask. Before leaving the apartment she threw on her eye shield: a pair of blacked-out Ray Bans rimmed with pointy metal studs. Her vision went black-and-white, matching the way she felt inside. Monotone and old.

The chill in the air when she stepped onto the street was welcoming. Bernadette shivered and held herself and began to walk, retracing her steps through the fog. Retracing their original steps together: to the store, to the beach, to the joy and back again, to return to her bed. This time however, she knew that she would be skipping the part of happiness.

Promise we'll be happy, today? Tristan had asked her the last time they walked together.

Today, we'll be happy, she'd said to him.

~

Bernadette entered *Hops & Vines Market* and smiled at the owner, Edgar, who had been a witness to their love. Many a time, she and Tristan had stumbled in loud and laughing, drunk on their love, their drinking, and sometimes their candy—their favorite powder candy they used to snort to numb themselves from the world and reality. The world, according to them, could always wait because it wasn't going anywhere but around and around in circles. No, they much preferred to be lost in one another. They were each other's favorite carousel.

Tristan and Bernadette would stand inside of the walk-in cooler entwined around one another as if they were a singular being and peruse the bottles, cans and cases of their favorite brews, seltzers, and elixirs. The last time they'd stood together there, he'd wrapped his arms around her to keep her warm, resting his chin on top of her head. *What do you feel like drinking?* She'd asked him. *Get whatever you want baby*, he said. *Oh…today I get whatever I want?* She laughed, while he kissed the side of her face. *You always get whatever you want*, he said, squeezing her tightly. *Oh do I? So today anything?*

~

"How are you today?" Edgar asked her.

He entered the cooler with a wooden crate of wine, set it down by her feet, and then straightened up and smiled at her kindly. Even through his grey-tinted eye shield Bernadette glimpsed the concern in his aquamarine eyes.

"I'm fine," she said, while grabbing her favorite bottle of cold dry rose-tinged wine, "about to get finer."

"Alright, just making sure," he said, opening the door for her.

Bernadette paid, said goodbye, and left, avoiding Edgar's gaze. She wondered if he could tell. *Can he see? Does he know? Do I need to start going somewhere else? Should I stop going out? Do I need to order a delivery service? No. No. He doesn't know. He just cares for his neighbors. It's okay. He doesn't know. He didn't see. He has his shield on, I have my shield on. It's okay.* She convinced herself to breathe, and kept walking.

~~

The theatre was cold on the evening the cast of Shakespeare's *Antony and Cleopatra* gathered on stage for the news. It was two hours before call time, for what was supposed to be their final tech rehearsal. Bernadette had been pouring sugar into her black coffee, when she first received the text to go to the theatre early. She'd shuddered when she heard that ding of her cellphone. She'd been listening to the radio all morning, which had only increased her confusion while simultaneously smiting her faith. Normally, the ritual of their warm-ups together cultivated golden warmth in the theatre and calmed Bernadette in a way no other thing could. That night however, she stood with the company in a frigid silence until their producer, Gayle, forlorn and exhausted and unable to meet their gazes, told them, "I'm sorry. We have to postpone the show. We'll let you all know. For now, go home."

The Cherimoya Syndrome was born in New York City. It began with the colleges: New York University, then Columbia, then SUNY Purchase. Then it was Cornell campus on Roosevelt Island, including many residents of the island. Then Broadway, then Wall Street, then the general masses. Before the theatre went dark, during those times of uncertainty, Bernadette would sit at bars in LA with her cast mates after rehearsal. They'd sip their drinks as they watched the news but it wasn't long before the vast majority of them learned to turn away from the televisions.

"That won't happen here. Too much vitamin D and weed in California to keep us straight. Winter sucks. Ughhhh—so glad I left New York forever ago. It's fucking miserable there, it's no wonder people are offing themselves... Shit was bound to hit the fan some fucking time," Gayle slurred while sipping on a dirty martini, her eyes glued to the screen, mesmerized by the chaos displayed: people jumping from buildings and people drowning themselves in the East River en masse. People running into oncoming trains and traffic. Students found hanging in their dorm rooms. Prisoners ramming their skulls into the concrete of their cells. Actors dropping from the mezzanine, snapping their necks on the center orchestra seats. People with slit wrists or multiple needles in their arms, rushed to the hospitals. The hospitals and clinics complete disaster areas. Very few were willing to admit the survivors of failed suicide for fear of following suite. The pain that the suicide survivors exuded was enough to frighten any doctor or nurse out of the room. It was the way the patients clutched at their chests, some of them digging their fingernails through the skin, as though trying to eradicate something. As if their hearts were on the verge of exploding. Few medical personnel had the courage to strap these survivors down and observe them.

The Cherimoya Syndrome swept across the East Coast; the death rates increased by the thousands daily. Soon enough, it would make its way West.

"It's not the cold," Bernadette said.

"It's like they're in a trance," said Tristan.

"Do you think we'll be okay?" she'd asked him, looking into his bright green eyes.

This was before it was presumed that the syndrome was spread by eye contact, and well before it became law to wear protective eye shields to prevent the spread of it. This was back when they communicated by stealing glances. He'd been the Antony to her Cleopatra then. She was in wonder at how hopeful yet lost he looked, although everything about him was inconsistent. He was engaged to somebody else, but the one certainty at that time of pure confusion, was that they had each other and they were falling in love for real.

Tristan took her hand. She could feel his love for her, Bernadette, pulsing in the palm of his hand.

"Together, we will be," he said.

~~

Bernadette reached the sand on Longest Beach. Other than the seagulls, the shore was void of any other living presence. The fog seemed to thin, and she took off her Ray Bans, blinking her eyes rapidly as they adjusted themselves to the greenish-grey tinge of the stinking Pacific Ocean. She reached into her fanny pack for her wine key and opened the bottle of rosé. Sighing as she swallowed straight from the bottle, she choked and laughed again. She laid herself on her back and let her mind wander into the sky. Wondering the letters 'W-H-Y' and staring up at the clouds, forming them into a cotton candy question.

"*Sir, I will eat no meat, I'll not drink, sir. If idle talk will once be necessary, I'll not sleep neither. This mortal house I'll ruin, do Caesar what he can,*" she whispered, alone, rehearsing her monologue for the show that never opened. Bernadette toyed with the wine key in her hand, sticking the corkscrew end in the sand. She closed her eyes and felt them burn from the tears she refused to cry. *Why fight it anymore,* she wondered, and closing her eyes again, she tried to remember why. There wasn't a reason. Desperately, she grabbed the bottle of wine by its neck and chugged the remaining rosy liquid. Then, gently, she pulled the wine key from the sand.

Bernadette traced the dull point of the corkscrew along the vertical lines that lived on her left wrist. Although she'd spent her career covering them up with makeup, the scars had been with her for her entire adult life. It was only fitting that it should end this way, for she was well versed in the act, despite the many years it had been since the last time she cut herself. Although this time, the final mark would certainly not be easy, in fact, it was definitely going to hurt. She suddenly wished she'd brought along a knife. Luckily, she remembered the flask full of vodka in her fanny pack, and used it to quell her frustration.

"Stupid. Useless. Even to the very end. Cheers, to you Bernadette!" she slurped from the flask and shouted up at the palm trees, pulling out a chunk of her baby hairs, and tossing them into the sand.

I loved the wrong man, she thought to herself, as she slumped back down into the sand. "Why couldn't you just pick me?!" she demanded to know, from the atmosphere, who was quiet to her plea. Bernadette shot back up onto her feet and began punching the air. With every fist thrown, a sob heaved in her chest. Then finally the tears began to flow, burning her entire face. She wept silently, clutching her heart as it pounded against the flesh and bones of her chest, threatening to burst. Falling back down to her knees, she decided she would just let the pain take over from there.

Suddenly a whistle sounded from the sea. Bernadette looked up from her misery, and spotted a familiar figure rising from the rippling tide. It was the cowboy, Alfred, from her recurring nightmare, horseback, riding the sterling stallion Silver Cotton Jimmy. She groaned, and then shouted, "GOD, you guys, AGAIN?!"

"Enough with the theatrics, Bernadette. I can feel you crumbling from here, woman!" Alfred called out to her, as he and Silver Cotton Jimmy shook off the stinging salt water.

"You stay over there!" Bernadette shouted, as she raised the empty wine bottle over her head, her brown eyes bulging out of their sockets menacingly. "I'm not in the mood, I'm warning you!"

Alfred and Silver Cotton Jimmy approached Bernadette steadfastly. Alfred rugged and blonde whiskered with smoldering grey eyes and Silver Cotton Jimmy glistening as though his coat and mane were of the finest pearly platinum. They left a trail of seaweed, used needles, potato chips bags, broken eye shields and plastic straws in their wake. "Calm down, Bernadette. We didn't come all this way for nothing," Alfred grunted. "We're here for you."

"I want to be alone. This is my place. You don't belong here," Bernadette said quietly, pointing the bottom of the bottle at Alfred's brain from a distance, as if deciding how to shoot her shot. Her legs shook beneath her and startled by her own frailty, she broke the wine bottle on the nearest palm tree and redirected her aim perilously, "Stay where you are. Don't come near me."

Alfred dismounted from Silver Cotton Jimmy, and raised his hands in the air as the stallion continued towards Bernadette with a gentle whinny, his tail shivering as he neared her. Bernadette lowered the jagged edged bottle, and Silver Cotton Jimmy nudged the side of her head and breathed out a hearty neigh, which calmed her. She dropped the broken bottle in the sand and took his head and mane into her own hands. Her falling teardrops glistened onto Silver Cotton Jimmy's face. He sighed against her body, and for a moment, the pain in her chest subsided. Bernadette buried herself in his warmth, forcing herself to remember.

~

Almonds. Tristan almost always smelled like vanilla clustered almonds. Like cyanide. He was the sweetest poison she'd ever known. She forgot all of her problems when they were together. She forgot herself, best of all. Bernadette never learned to love herself. But in loving Tristan, she convinced herself that it didn't matter.

Bernadette remembered most of their final day together. Two bottles of rosé for her. A bottle of Chardonnay for him. A bottle of Cabernet for them. A Carnage mug, a robot vacuum cleaner, hours of conspiracy theories, *Fight Club* by Chuck Palahniuk, *Dark Phoenix* the movie, 3 UFC classics, three sing-alongs, a freezing cold hotel room, one king sized bed, talk about hidden treasure on a Nova Scotian Island, kisses on her neck, kisses from their mouths, hundreds of kisses without disconnection, tongues entwining, pure satisfaction, belonging, rejection, him telling her how he knew his fiancé wasn't the one but how he'd made a promise and he had to fulfill it, her telling him why she never met anyone, because of him. And how she wished he'd promised her instead. An 8-ball of cocaine, his peachy keen flesh, her terracotta skin, their embrace, their connection. Then separating and severing limbs and her heading back to Longest Beach, ashamed, without him. He had made his choice. He was not going to go with her. She would have to learn how to stand without him, her reoccurring condition.

Alfred held Bernadette as she came to from her reverie. "Let's get up and walk," he said, lifting her up from the sand. Silver Cotton Jimmy followed alongside them. The fog had cleared, yet the sky remained clouded, from all of her questions. There was still so much to figure out.

"Sorry I yelled at you, Alfred." Bernadette said. "I've been so afraid."

"You need to learn how to manage your sadness."

"I don't know that I can. I caught the Cherimoya, and he couldn't love me, Alfred. It wasn't easy anymore," she said. "I was a fool. He never picked me to begin with. And then he saw it in my eyes, and he wouldn't risk it. He couldn't look at me anymore. He knew, and he was too afraid to try. But he's alive! He's alive! Without me. And I'm here and I'm nothing," she said, crying, laughing. "It's over. I've made a fool of myself. What can I do?"

"What can you do with your sadness?" Alfred asked. "Well, I'll tell you what I do! I dip mine in honey, and I swallow it!"

"Alfred, seriously—"

"You want to get serious, Bernadette?" Alfred ceased walking. "You know your options. You have not come to terms with them."

"I don't know. I've forgotten who I am," she insisted. "I want to remember. But I don't want to be here anymore. I don't think that I can do both."

Alfred said to her, "Listen. I've got my pistol. I've got this knife. I've even got some rope if you'd prefer to be strung up from this tree. You make a choice now. You live, or you don't. Hell, you don't think you can be here anymore? Me and Silver Cotton Jimmy will welcome you to our home. But we're not gonna keep chasing you around. You can keep hating yourself. Or you can start over. But stop feeling sorry for yourself. Stop sacrificing yourself. You are no lamb."

Bernadette looked into the eyes of the man and the creature from her nightmares and wondered what it would be like to dream again. To put an end to the haunting nightmares, and live past the fear, and conquer her sadness. To not continue to waste away, alone. To be herself again.

"Is there any work for an actress, where you're from?" she asked them.

"We always make time for entertainment in the Wild West," Alfred said, his moustache curling upwards, Silver Cotton Jimmy whinnying in agreement.

Alfred hoisted Bernadette upon Silver Cotton Jimmy, and they began the march back from where they came, across the sand, and into the tide. The pain in Bernadette's heart began to dwindle, as Alfred held the reins around her, enveloping her with protection. A measure of fear remained within her, yet the warmth of the silver steed beneath her thighs was enough for her to brave the depths before them. They descended into the sea. Bernadette's hair billowed downwards, dragging her under, and she smiled. She was free now. She was beginning to start over.

-Meredith Miranda

-Eddie Jelinet

Vertical

On y voit plus grand-chose
Du décor initial

Des garçonnières gluantes
Effondré au velux
la corde est sensible
Assurément

On m'a vendu un été interminable et des temps de
communication à ne plus savoir qu'en foutre
On m'a vendu des vérandas plus vaste que le monde
On m'a vendu du sexe à en exploser
On m'a vendu des sourires éblouissants et un groupe
d'ami en lunettes de soleil, licenciés en droit, Taille M
et photos de vacances à Copacabana
On ma vendu un amour inconditionnel aussi

On peut vendre tout un tas de trucs à un être humain
Quand il est seul
Et sans espoir

La corde est sensible

On y voit plus grand-chose
À travers les lucarnes
Une terre de ferraille et de verres brisés

Le regard est une blessure ouverte
Qu'on ne peut cautériser
La vérité se fige
comme une maladie grave

La corde sensible
La corde mineure
La corde raide

Et le dernier mot
à la

V
E
R
T
I
C
A
L

-Grégoire Parville

Numero 1

Espejismos de dulce vanidad
con sabor a canela y miel.
Ecos de risas
que se difuminan
en el recuerdo del tiempo.
Sabores que jamás
volverán a ser degustados.
Susurro cálido
nunca más escuchado.
Palabras hechas de vapor de hiel,
de veneno caramelizado.
Caricias pretéritas,
mudas las memorias,
en blanco y negro observado.
Tus ojos ya no me buscan
y tus manos esquivas,
ya no me tocan,
de mi se han alejado.
Paso que extingue
el sendero empolvado por la vida.
Niebla en cascada,
te cubre,
solitaria en el horizonte.
Aquella promesa incumplida

y aquel cálido tarareo
hoy no es sino humo de leño quemado.
De brasas consumidas
mezcladas con lluvia y barro.
Momento que se despeña,
desprendido de la retina,
caído en combate insulso,
idiota,
infantil y funesto.
Como tormenta de arena
ocultando el desierto de lo prohibido,
por orgullo y miedo,
sepultado el amor.
Inocencia envenenada,
penitencia enamorada,
desamparada la cordura,
de embuste se viste la certeza.
Melodía arrinconada,
de acordes desmontada,
carente,
insípida,
difuminada en el reflejo que te contempla.

Hoy no reconozco mis actos,
mis vocablos,
forastero de mis versos,
a dónde fue lo predilecto,
lo idolatrado.
Puertas cerradas,

petardos mojados,
hierba marchita,
disecada,
pensamiento de piedra labrado.
Perdido el tacto
entre preguntas espinadas
retórica sofocada,
disparatada determinación,
la nada nos contempla.

-Erick Szczurek

Unraveling

I pricked a hole in the hollow of our love
i stabbed the hot air balloon that housed us with a
pen, i
pulled out the bathtub drain too early
while we were still in it
soaking
resting
enjoying,
i
cleared a pristine painted vase off the edge of a glass
nightstand
with my clumsy flailing arm
while i was half asleep,
i
barreled my boat into the fragile stems of a nearly
beaten down dam,
pillars that were barely holding on, maybe,
had a year or two on them left, maybe,
yet whom were not ready to go quite yet.

i am the reason this vessel is now
deflating
draining
bleeding out

crashing down,
shattering into chards too fine
to collect or sweep,
crumbling to nothing more than
splintered logs, debris and dust.

i thought we had more time.
i would've given anything for more time.

nothing feels more alone
than sleeping next to someone
who is beginning to fall out of love with you.
nothing feels more alone
than trying to memorize the smell of his neck
in case this is the last time he ever holds you.

who knew it would only take seven simple words:
"i'm not ever going to want kids."

-Lavender Malin

-*Eddie Jelinet*

Voz pretérita,
cansada, lapidaria.
Las palabras de su boca nacen vacías,
sin fundamentos,
forradas de vulgar lamento,
pero como cuchillos, afiladas.
Aliento tóxico,
nuclear,
la dulzura de un te quiero
a años luz de sus labios.
Mirada de quebrantahuesos
te observa envolvente
encapotando el sol,
erizándote con sus gélidas pupilas.
Desde más arriba del hombro,
falaz superioridad.
Actitud que devasta
con su onda expansiva,
como asteroide en colisión,
fulminando la existencia de la vida
con un chascarrillo entre sus dientes.
Las edades del hombre
soportan sus pisadas
de caminar tosco,

despojando de sueños
a quien bajo su credo no se somete.
Apisonando corazones inocentes
de los que se alimenta
al convertirlos en papilla.
Chantaje, victimismo,
doble y tercer sentido,
manipulación,
lágrimas de cartón calculadas
según conveniencia.
Impotente en el amar,
cegada de ira,
apología de la vida repetida,
científica,
cuadriculada.
En el confort de un salón
con mesa cargadita de manjares
que en hiedras que se enredan
al masticarlos se convierten
estrangulándote desde dentro.
Agonía sin sentido,
empuje sin cerebro.
Fascismo emocional,
impedimento racional,
arte enterrado antes de nacer,
sofocante academicismo,
vagina de granito,
poesía desventurada
impregnada de grasa animal.

Montaña etílica,
foresta blanquecina
crece en su loma,
sin clorofila,
sin fotosíntesis,
cautiva de nefasto pensamiento,
fantasma de otro tiempo,
erradicada la familia,
arrancado el sentimiento,
facturas y pantomimas,
verduras caras y resentimiento.
Ante ella, el correr veloz,
lejos,
un alivio es,
una obligación,
un mandamiento.
No abandonarme a su merced,
no satisfacer su loca tozudez,
no averiguar cuan cruel puede ser,
no continuar con esta desfachatez.
La soledad,
el silencio de sus sombras,
crucificada vida patética
alontanada de un abrazo sincero.
Al final, lástima siento,
de quien pudo ser y no fue
y aunque no entiendas estas palabras
te deseo paz y un te quiero...

-Erick Szczurek

Love Relations

"Magnetism: a physical phenomenon produced by the motion of electric charge, resulting in attractive and repulsive forces between objects."

A formidable magnet, like the earth, is in coordinated, synchronized flow. It is billions of electrons moving, forming charged currents, all arranging and twirling and coordinating direction and then clustering into pools and streams and rivers of microscopic particles. Magnetism, polarity, repulsion, attraction, all part of a fluid dance of moving energy, aligning then re-aligning.

When this dance is interrupted or disturbed, when these particles become disorderly or chaotic–if the movement of these electrons are no longer in synchronized flow and agreement, the magnetic field is weakened or lost, the magnet no longer magnetic.

~

Last night during the concert, a cute guy tried to pick me up. His hair was pulled back into a ponytail with dreadlocks hanging at the back of his neck. His eyes were bright and lazy like evening sunlight and I liked the way he smiled at me, a little tipsy but mostly enchanted.

"Tu es vraiment tres belle," he both laughed

and stated. "Si tu étais ma copine, chaque jour je te ferais l'amour. Vraiment, je t'aime. Tu es avec quelqu'un?" I nodded my head, "Oui, je suis avec quelqu'un…"
"Oahhh le mec, il a vraiment de la chance, putain." He looked at me in that appreciative way…

With his innocent smile and bold sincerity, he charmed me. "Moi, je dis ce que je pense…" he said, unapologetic. I let his hand rest a little on my arm before shrugging into some distance. I stared at him coyly.

It was nice to play along for a while, as though it mattered, as though it were true, as though it were more than a silly thing that "people just say" when they've had a few drinks. "I would make love to you everyday." I smiled and giggled at the idea.

Maybe for a while he would make love to me everyday, for a while…until he started noticing all the things he didn't quite like about me. Until I got sad, or got mad, or became difficult in some way. Or until I became too habitual, or uncomfortable, or inconvenient…until he started thinking that I'm not that special, that's I'm no longer fun and actually he's sort of maybe just needing something different…until one night we go out, go to see a concert, and he stands by my side looking out at all of the other dancing, charming girls and thinking, "wow, if I had her, if *she* were my girlfriend, I'd make love to her everyday."

-A.Gallagher

If We Got Married
(or the Armenian girl's lament)

If we got married,
I'd wear crystal slippers
And hang empty bottles from my ears
I'd let you fill them with your thoughts
So my head could sink into my spine
I'd tiptoe quietly at night
And sound like twinkling lights,
And definitely forget how compressed
My little feet are.
If we got married,
I'd sing some eggs up for you in the mornings,
Draw the curtains and swallow the sun
And definitely keep smiling
Even though five thousand seven hundred seventy-
eight kelvins
Are burning me up from inside.
If we got married,
I'd tape my mouth
And let you steal kisses.
I'd give you my breasts and my womb
And definitely remain tiny and firm
Especially after your first, second, third, fourth son
is born.

If we got married,
(I'd castrate you with obedience)
I'd choke you with stoicism
Tie a quiet noose around your thick neck
Trip on the stool underneath your feet
Contemplate the tiles
Chop some beets
And definitely sign the papers for divorce.

-*Tamara Sevunts*

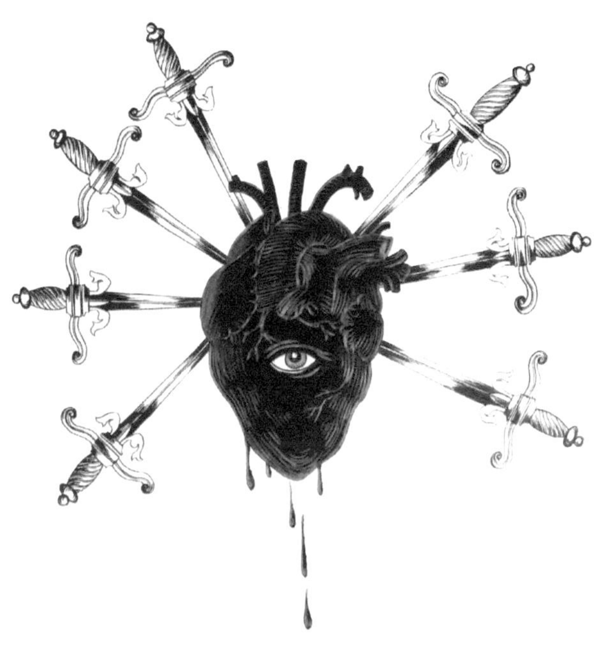

-Eddie Jelinet

Qué Se Yo

Me piden que hable del Amor y me da por recordar pero no sé bien qué opinar. Quizás me pueda parecer que el Amor es ese regalo mentiroso que Dios nos envió para así perpetrar la especie o quizás es ese mar donde te zambulles para convertirte en eterno líquido, y así, fluir natural. Quizás sea una flor espinada que te desangrará si de su fragancia tu jardín quieres llenar o quizás sea brisa que te envuelve como a la hoja seca, elevándola alto, hasta abrazar al firmamento. Tantas traiciones pavimentan su sendero pedregoso, tantas veces chubascos de lágrimas se derramaron sobre su océano de sueños rotos, donde en su costa, un aire gélido menea allí los árboles del bosque de los besos que no se dieron, pero quizás sea también cada nacimiento, bautizado con ese primer beso de madre entregada cuando entre sus brazos, sostiene a su recién alumbrado hij@.

Puede ser que el Amor, viejo burlón ciego, se permita llenarte de las mariposas de la ilusión tu estómago. Por su nombre el censo del campo santo llena sus páginas de tragedias eternas que nos conmueven al leerlas, al identificarnos con ellas. Porque su gotear caprichoso, el de éste néctar delicioso, es tan antiguo como el mundo. Y lo beberás voluntariamente si eres digno de arrimar su sagrado cáliz a tus labios. Porque el Amor te aproxima a Dios, a su divina creación de la cual eres sólo la millonésima parte de su proyecto, pero a su vez fuiste creado a su imagen y semejanza. El Amor es su bendición, y tu sentirás su mano posándose en tu corazón cuando toque a la puerta de tu hogar.

El Amor no se compra ni se vende, no se secuestra ni obedece al miedo o al egoísmo. Es un pájaro que luce virginal plumaje dorado pero a su vez posee robustas garras que despedazarán tu alma si no te encuentra capaz de volar junto a él con devoción y alegría, porque te coronará monarca o te empujará a sus oscuras mazmorras hasta convertirte en el fósil de lo que una vez fue un humano libre.

El Amor es una sonrisa sincera, un susurro cálido próximo a tu cuello, es un manto camaleónico, una antorcha que ilumina al mundo desde el primer día de su creación, y tu eres su honorable huésped. Tu eres una nota en el pentagrama de su melodía. Es la onda expansiva que devasta tu ignorancia y tu esterilidad. El Amor sostiene cada pisada de tu cuerpo, es cada partícula de oxígeno exhalada por ti, es cada fruto regalado por el generoso árbol de la vida, cada caricia del Sol y cada guiño furtivo de la plateada Luna, es el cantar de una chicharra en verano, el aroma de la hierba mojada o el sabor de la maracuyá cuando está madura, la mirada dulce de tu abuela, el consejo del padre reposado, la lamida de tu perro, la leche de la vaca preñada, la orilla de la playa besándote en cada vaivén de su balanceo, con la arena permitiéndote hacer garabatos de tus sueños con una rama que flotó hasta llegar a tu mano, es la voz de la noche, de grillos, calor, de ramaje acariciado por el viento del sur, la primera vez que tu ser amado te dio la mano, agitándote con su cósmica mirada y derritiéndote cuando poso sus labios junto a los tuyos. El Amor de labrar la tierra donde diseminaste las semillas del porvenir.

Quizás el Amor sea la verdadera energía que nos empuja hasta el final del trayecto para así trascender de nivel de manera adecuada, y su ausencia, nos desvincula del camino hacia Dios.

Quizás... Qué se yo…

-Erick Szczurek

Este cuento fue inspiración de la madre Tierra en Lamas, Perú.

Imagina girar y girar
como los niños
jugando en el patio
Imagina girar y girar
como hacíamos
en el columpio de la escuela
Imagina rodar
como una rueda
bajando la cuesta del monte…

Mira,
en la selva
las hormigas suben y suben
suben hasta lo más alto del árbol
hacia el cielo
aunque el desafío
les pueda llevar a la muerte

Sin embargo
suben
como si estuvieran en un trance.
Marchan

hacia arriba
dominados por el impulso
inescapable causa
de un invisible invasor
polvo de un hongo venenoso

las hormigas corren
hasta la cima del árbol
solo para caer a la muerte
algunos logran caer vivos
solo para volver a subir
de nuevo

La justicia es eminente

sabías que la velocidad de la luz
es frecuencia? sonido?
música de las esferas?
Siempre busca girar
en perfecta harmonía.
danza infinita.

La justicia es eminente
siempre volvemos a la luz.

-MAJA

Llámame Negra

Yo tengo dos lados en mi sangre y nadie sabe, parece que nadie quiere saber...
Este cuerpo mío, en dentro de cada célula, está escrito la experiencia de mis antepasados de mis antecesores y los de ellos.
Guerra, violación, muerte, liberación, nacimiento, amor, pena, sufrimiento.
Mi cuerpo es una memoria: un compuesto de lo que ya pasó, del aquí y ahora, y de tanta posibilidad lo que llamamos el futuro.

Mis padres, y los de ellos, aquellos que fueron conquistados, que fueron esclavos, que han sido violado, robado—su historia está escrita en mi, está aquí conmigo..
Mis padres, y los de ellos, aquellos que conquistaron, que violaron, que robaron, que torturaron—su historia aquí esta escrita, está aquí conmigo.

O! Pena de esclavitud!
O! pena de libertad!
O! Pena de mis huesos que han perdido sus restos.
O! Pena del árbol de mi sangre que ya no mas tiene raíces, que ya no mas tiene tierra tierna.

O! pena de mis hermanos, O! pena de mis hermanas.
Tu historia, aquí conmigo, tus traumas, aquí en mi
piel, por dentro y por fuera, aquí están escrito!

Entonces llámame negra, que me da más fuerza.
Llámame negra, porque hablar de lo Negro es hablar
de lo Blanco.
Llámame mestiza porque soy el medio de dos lados.
Llámame Taino porque en mi sangre
mis ancestros viven.
Llámame morena porque soy de la tierra.
Sangre azul del mar, piel de café,
valles de mango entre mis pies.
Soy humana, soy viviente,
soy la fuerza que une este puente.

Llámame negra, que me da más fuerza.
Llámame negra.

-A.Gallagher

This World Is Trouble

Faut qu'on trace vite, la morale s'agite,
les règles sont tacites, la rage implicite,
les parents nous salissent bébé, les amis trahissent,
on les baisera tous, on s'aimera tout seul,
faut qu'ça glisse.
C'est chaud pour les clitoris, désolé mon amour
j'arrêterais pas l'vice,
je nique la police à m'en faire péter l'pas d'vis,
dans ce monde de bites y'a qu'les culs qui rougissent.
Tous des esclaves mais t'as le droit de subir,
avale, étouffe et bave mais garde le sourire.
On est tous esclave mais t'as le droit d'sévir,
matraquent, éborgnent et violent mais se font élire.

Même si je dois les tuer un par un,
t'inquiète pas pour tous ces humains.
On les enterrera dans le jardin,
et on fera l'amour jusqu'à demain, tout ira bien.

This world is trouble but we'll be okay.

T'es pas né au bon endroit au bon moment,
t'es pas né de la bonne couleur ou du bon sang,
t'es pas née du bon sexe ou du bon rang,

Itachi, Joker, Assange, mes héros banc d'méchants.
Quoi que l'on fasse on se suit à la trace,
de l'étiquette à l'oreille à l'étiquette à l'orteil.
Dans le ventre de la bête on se bat pour des miettes
aux oubliettes…
Laissons les s'entre-tuer, laisse tu sais le temps va trier.
Rien à faire pour les fumer, laisse tu sais les bancs
vont brûler.
Arrête de tout calculer, laisse les cancres vont briller,
je suis trop calé, décalé, laisse le tendre va vriller.
T'inquiète on va bien s'caler, laisse les glands vaciller,
j'ai tous scanné ils vont juste tous caner.

Même si j'dois les tuer un par un,
t'inquiète pas pour tous ces humains.
On les enterrera dans le jardin,
Et on fera l'amour jusqu'à la fin, tout ira bien.

This world is trouble but we'll be okay

-el Malotonio

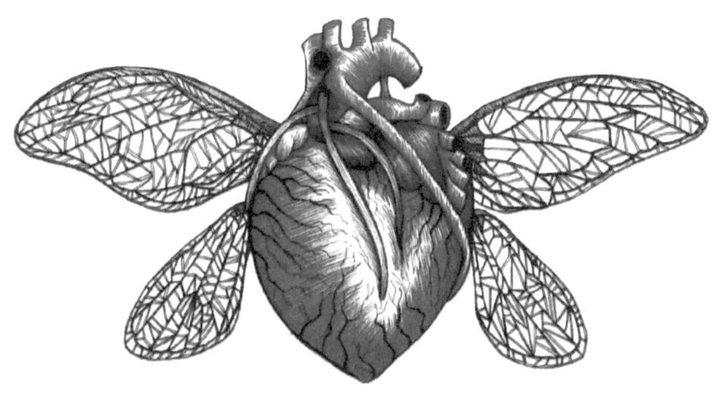

-Eddie Jelinet

Numero 12

Mustia y vacía,
tristemente invariable,
previsible en tu discurso,
bañado de líquida angustia,
cristalina como la mirada de tu muerte.
Contaminas lo que nombras,
construyes castillos
con ladrillos de sangre,
te disfrazas con la sombra,
eres nefasta en todo lo que haces.
Te divierten las desgracias
y con ellas alimentas tu verbo
que al ser escuchado
tímpanos en oídos deshace.
Como mantequilla los derrite
tu logodiarrea te complace,
tu sonrisa engaña al inocente,
tu gestos enloquecen al observarte.
Destilas bromuro con tus mentiras,
tus labios maldicen al cruzarse
porque de tu boca nacen espinas
que ponzoñosas se clavan como estandartes.
Y de tu malicia ni los vientos escapan,
el tiempo se detiene a contemplarte

porque en estatua de sal te conviertes
al sentir los vapores que de tu hálito nacen.
La falsedad te viste noche y día
y tu tranquilidad augura mal desenlace
porque de lo que siembras recoges
y quien siembra tormentas
recoge tempestades.
Cuan vulgares son tus victorias,
cuan pobres son tus vergüenzas,
cuan famélicas las vacas de tu leche,
cuan tristes tus vanidades.
Piedad y benevolencia
sean levantados en sus lugares,
que sea aplacada tu turbia existencia
y sea transformado todo aquello que te place,
en luz de mediodía,
en brisa de verano abrazando a los amantes.

-Erick Szczurek

Sirenita Del Mar

En un pueblo costero
Viví una sirenita morena
De unos rizos largos
Remolino de pelo algas marina.
Se pierde entre huesos
De rocas
caracol
Crujiente
crustáceos.
Resbala entre dos aguas
Deslizas
Viajando
Como ballena azul
Con ojos despiertos
Reflejo de luz
Luminaria cósmica
Sol, luna y estrellas.
Ballena solitaria
Sirenita
Secuestrada
Entre lo más profundo
De la arena
En el fondo de los mares.
Sabe algo que vos

Solo sabrás
En oír
Sus bellas canciones.
Escucha...

-Tormenta Azul

Between You And The Sea

To all future lovers who will seek my heart,
on account of all past lovers who didn't understand
why they couldn't keep it,
floating in a glass jar of water,
fresh and alive,
once they acquired it:

i can promise that i will love you
as deep
as true
as far
as i can
to the best of my human ability.
but honey
don't
please don't
ask me to choose
between you and the sea.

for if you did,
for if i were forced to make
an impossible choice,
i would have to break your heart.

for the sea is my spirit
the sea is my soul, my life, my breath,
and just as the trees are my oxygen,
and just as the road is my sustenance,
the sea will never
not be a part of me.

and let me ask you this --
would you make a woman choose
between you and her skin?
would you ask a deer to choose
between you and her drink of water?
would you make a fish choose
between you and the lake?
would you ask a goddess to choose
between you and the sky?
would you ask the sun to choose
between you
and her light?

-Lavender Malin

Contents

Forward (Rebellious Thoughts) 7
  -A. Gallagher
El Elixir   13
  -MAJA
I Only Feel Safe When It's Toxic 17
  -Lavender Malin
Numero 5   21
  -Erick Szczurek
Remplir Le Vide   25
  -el Malotonio
Ode   29
  -Lavender Malin
Love to the Brown-Skin Girl   31
  -A. Gallagher
C'est Un Beau et Triste Monde 37
  -Grégoire Parville
Censured   45
  -Tamara Sevunts
Numero 7   49
  -Erick Szczurek
La Colère Qui Fuse   51
  -el Malotonio
"Those Who Think They Are Above Animals…" 55
  -A.Gallagher
Worth 59
  -Roe Taylor

Petites Pensées Pesantes73
  -Tamara Sevunts
Rebecca Landi 75 - 81
Some Things I Think About When I...   83
  -A. Gallagher
Cherimoya   87
  -Meredith Miranda
Vertical   103
  -Grégoire Parville
Numero 1   105
  -Erick Szczurek
Unraveling   109
  -Lavender Malin
Numero 13   113
  -Erick Szczurek
Love Relations 117
  -A.Gallagher
If We Got Married   119
  -Tamara Sevunts
Qué Se Yo   123
  -Erick Szczurek
Cuentos De La Selva   127
  -MAJA
Llámame Negra   129
  -A.Gallagher
This World Is Trouble 131
  -el Malotonio
Numero 12   135
  -Erick Szczurek

Sirenita Del Mar   137
   -Tormenta Azul
Between You And The Sea   139
   -Lavender Malin

Eddie Jelinet Artwork
23, 35, 47, 57, 101, 111, 121, 133

*Many thanks to everyone who participated
in this publication.*

*For more information about this book
and its contributors please
visit labrujaonline.com*

La Bruja
-independent publishing sin fronteras-